The Trusted Leader

Understanding the
Trust Triangle

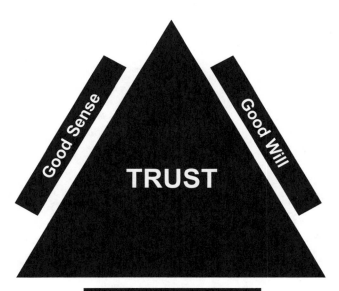

Steve Gladis, Ph.D.

Foreword by Marshall Goldsmith

HRD Press, Inc. • Amherst. •. Massachusetts

Published by: HRD Press, Inc.
22 Amherst Road
Amherst, MA 01002
413-253-3488
800-822-2801 (U.S. and Canada)
413-253-3490 (fax)
www.hrdpress.com

ISBN 978-1-59996-204-7

Editorial services by Sally Farnham
Production services by Jean Miller
Cover design by Eileen Klockars

Dedication

This book is dedicated to my grandson, Jake Diaz, as he grows and learns about the importance of earning trust from the "coaches" in his own life.

Table of Contents

Foreword

Trust is among the most important words in the vocabulary of leadership. With trust, there's not much you can't get done. Without it, even the smartest people in the world can get little done. Trust speeds up progress, and progress drives both happiness and meaning—core concepts of my own research and my new book: *MOJO: How to Get It, How to Keep It, How to Get It Back If You Lose It.*

In *The Trusted Leader*, Steve Gladis does several things very well. First, he helps the reader clearly frame and visualize the basic concept of trust. Using the structure of The Trust Triangle and adapting Aristotle's bedrock theory of trustworthiness (good character, good sense, and good will), the author makes the sometimes elusive concept of trust far more concrete and definable, thus attainable.

Second, the author fleshes out the detail to make The Trust Triangle have more substance and depth. An analysis of these deeper elements (the 5 C's, the 5 K's, and the 5 H's) is supported by well-established research in the field of leadership. For example, Daniel Goleman's work on emotional and social intelligence, Bob Cialdini's work on influence, and Jim Kouzes and Barry Posner's research on leadership are all relevant to Gladis' Trust Triangle.

Third, the concept of the business leadership fable is emerging as a legitimate teaching genre. Steve Gladis has a gift for integrating useful theory and scholarship into an artful story that feels like you're watching a screenplay unfold in your mind, not trekking through a densely written textbook—hoping and praying for the last page. You can read this book in less than a couple of hours and retain the lessons because the key information is hung on the structure of a well-crafted story. This is a book I can and will recommend to clients in search of what makes good leadership work: Trust.

Marshall Goldsmith

Marshall Goldsmith is a leading executive coach and world authority in helping leaders improve. The author of numerous books, including *New York Times* best-seller *What Got You Here Won't Get You There*, his most recent is: *MOJO: How to Get It, How to Keep It, How to Get it Back if You Lose It* (2010). Marshall has won numerous prestigious awards including being recently recognized as one of the fifteen most influential business thinkers in the world in the 2009 bi-annual study sponsored by *The (London) Times* and *Forbes*.

Introduction

Without trust, no relationship can survive, let alone thrive. Above all others, leaders must understand how trust works, what its components are, how to build trust, and how you can lose trust.

The basic research for this book goes back more than 2,000 years to the seminal writings of Aristotle, perhaps one of the greatest minds of all times. Aristotle posited that for speakers to be credible and trustworthy, they had to have three characteristics—Good Character, Good Sense and Good Will.

1. **Good Character** was central to credibility in Aristotle's schema and is the basis for what I call The Trust Triangle. And central to character is honesty. The simple question we all ask ourselves when we meet someone new, especially a new leader, is this: Can I believe this person?

2. **Good Sense** was the second pillar in Aristotle's theory and is the second leg of The Trust Triangle. It's not enough to just be honest; great leaders have to be competent in their own right (i.e., in their areas of expertise).

3. **Good Will** was the final pillar of Aristotle's theory and is the third leg of The Trust Triangle. Great leaders have to show others that they have their best interests at heart. Leaders must guard the welfare of others and reach out beyond themselves toward a higher cause—the team.

All three aspects of this triangle of Good Character, Good Sense, and Good Will must be present to produce a great, trustworthy leader. Leaders who possess strengths in only one or even two sides of the triangle will not succeed over time. In essence, without support from all three sides of the triangle, it (and leaders themselves) will collapse. This principle is easy to comprehend but harder to implement.

This leadership fable, *The Trusted Leader,* is the story of a young leader, Carlos Lopez, who gets promoted to supervise his former peers — no easy feat for any emerging leader. For example, he gets conflicting advice from his boss about how to take charge, and it backfires. Confused and uncertain, he seeks out the best leader he's ever known: his former high-school basketball coach, Jack Dempsey. The two agree to meet regularly to talk about leadership at a local restaurant. In a way, it's like *Tuesdays with Morrie* , Mitch Albom's celebrated best seller.

The Coach teaches Carlos how to lead, while Carlos and the Coach learn about each other's secret, sad, but ultimately formative pasts. Finally, the Coach teaches Carlos about The Trust Triangle — the critical key to leadership. The final chapter of the book describes the details of The Trust Triangle and is the basis for the leadership workshops that I teach on the subject of trust to companies and organizations.

I wish you luck on your personal leadership journey.

Steve Gladis

Chapter 1
Tossing Up a Jump Ball

Carlos Lopez arrived at the offices of Johnson, Talon, and Sorrento (JTS) every day by 7:30 A.M. but never before Jim Talon, the only remaining named partner, who seemed to live at the office. Thirty years old, Carlos stood six feet two, had jet black hair, a smooth olive complexion, and a soft demeanor that made women swoon when he was around, and men a bit jealous, though he was far too likeable to infuse any sense of lasting ill will.

When Carlos walked by Jim's office, he poked his head in the doorway and said, "Hi, Jim." Looking up over his bifocals, Jim held up his hand to say hello and satisfy the social greeting. The physical opposite of Carlos, Jim was sixty, bald, white, stout, and crusty, and Carlos knew better than to try to engage the man who was in the thick of reading *The Washington Post, The Wall Street Journal,* and *The New York Times* almost simultaneously – the three of them spread out on the long conference table in his office. Jim was widely considered the strategic genius of the firm because he scoured the media, intelligence reports, and any analytics available to him like a bloodhound following the scent of a missing person.

So Carlos headed for his desk, just outside the manager's office which he would be occupying soon as JTS's newest consultant practice manager. His promotion had not been made official despite the fact that rumors were buzzing about like a thousand gnats on a hot and humid summer's day. Carlos looked at the other name plates on the desks near his: Mary Cotton, Roger Barstow, and Janice Rollins. While he read each name plate, Carlos thought that his colleagues certainly had their strengths and their challenges. Mary Cotton, 29 years old, was a great writer and wrote all the team's reports; she also had a very different view of work and craved flexibility—almost to a fault. Roger Barstow, 42, was the best analyst in the entire office but was intolerant of people who were not in his intellectual league. And Janice Rollins, 54, was a workhorse and a longtime employee as well as the COG (Chief Office Gossip). Fortunately, Carlos had learned to work with each of them, so there would be few surprises, or so he thought.

Carlos had been at his desk for about a half-hour, well before the others had started to trickle in, when Jim called him into his office, which was a bit of a Marine Corps shrine. Jim had been an officer in Vietnam and got out in the early 1970s after the war began to draw to a close. One whole corner of his office was devoted to the Marine Corps, including a couple of rows of medals in a shadow box, a twilight picture of the Iwo Jima flag raising, and five plaques and pictures, all in gold frames. Mounted on the wall above all the memorabilia was Jim's Marine Corps silver and gold dress sword—as if standing guard above the shrine.

After Carlos took a seat in front of Jim's desk, Jim began to discuss the economy, which seemed to dominate most conversations these days. He was concerned about meeting the company's revenue projections, though many of their clients were government agencies and government contractors and thus a bit protected from the economic storm. Still, uncertainty and risk swirled around every business these days, he explained to a listening Carlos. Toward the end of his near-monologue, Jim said, "Well, today I'm sending out a release promoting you to manager."

Carlos just looked at him and then down at the floor. "OK, I guess it's a good time?"

"I'm not hearing a lot of conviction in your voice, Carlos."

"I just…"

"You concerned about the team?"

"Yes."

"They'll get used to it in time. Trick is, you have to go in and show them who's in charge. Like an alpha dog marking his territory."

"Tough image to hold, especially after a couple of cups of coffee!"

Jim roared with laughter and hit the desk with his hand. "But I'm serious. Go in hard, and if you get any opposition, crush it."

"Really?"

"Yep, someone will test you early on. Put the hammer down, or you'll be playing catch up for the rest of your time in the job."

"But, I'm not you," Carlos replied.

"Not yet, of course, but you'll learn."

"But…"

Jim cut him off, now leaning in with a stare that felt white hot to Carlos, "Look Carlos, either you want this opportunity or not. Are you in?"

Pausing only slightly, Carlos agreed, "I'm in." He had worked for Jim and seen his command-and-control style succeed over the years. No one ever crossed Jim and remained at the firm to talk about it.

"Great. You get any problems, let me know, but I'm sending this announcement e-mail out this morning, appointing you to the management team." With that, Jim stood up, stuck out his hand, vice-gripped Carlos' hand in his own, and shook it with vigor.

"First order of business is for you to move into your new office before the rest of your crew gets here," Jim said. "Good time to mark your territory."

"You sure that's a good idea? Maybe I should wait a day or two for it to sink in. George has only been retired a week now."

"All the more reason for you to push his stuff out and your stuff in. Time to claim your office. Make it yours, Carlos. George is gone."

"OK. if you think it's best. I'm just...."

"Go for it. I've got to get back to work," Jim said, pointing to the stack of files on his desk.

"OK. Thanks, Jim."

Carlos walked back to his desk with slow, deliberate steps. He pulled open the top desk drawer and looked at its contents for a while before he started to clean it out into an empty box that he'd found in the copy room last week.

When he'd finished, Carlos carried the box to "George's office" and set it down on the desk. It felt weird to him to enter that space. Like a boy trying out his father's easy chair, Carlos sat in the same worn leather chair that George Hampton had rocked in whenever Carlos or the other team members had explained a problem to their revered, wise boss. There were still nail holes in the office walls and bright spots that had been covered by George's pictures and artifacts, which had hung for two decades. Two dark blue wing chairs faced the heavy mahogany desk. Carlos remembered sitting in these chairs many times and taking pages of notes as George held forth like a modern-day Socrates.

Carlos looked out the window that allowed light to spill in and warm his face. When he opened his eyes, he spotted Janice getting out of her car and walking toward the front of the building. His pulse began to speed up. His immediate instinct was to walk out of the office so that it would not appear that he was poaching the not-yet-cold chair, but he remembered what Jim had said about establishing his territory, so he remained in the creaky old chair behind the desk and appeared to be settling in—albeit with a near-empty desk.

Janice was drawn to the light of Carlos' new office like a dog to a hydrant. Without being invited, she walked right into the office, looked around and then at Carlos, and said, "What's going on?"

Carlos looked up from the papers he'd just unloaded. "Hey, Janice. I'm, well….Jim is sending out an e-mail this morning."

"Let me guess. You're the new George."

"Well, yes, I guess…I'm… I'll have… Well, I will be the new manager."

"I knew it!" she said as if she'd won the lottery. With that she left the office as fast as her thick legs would carry her large frame and made a beeline for her computer.

Damn, Carlos thought.

Chapter 2
Recruiting the Coach

Jack Dempsey sat in the living room of his three-bedroom rambler in the Aura Hills subdivision of Arlington, Virginia, reading *The Washington Post* when a fly distracted him and he looked up. As he did, his eyes met the picture of Martha, his deceased wife. He stared at her smiling face — when she was young and gorgeous — the year he'd first started coaching basketball at Arlington High School in 1967.

The retired coach got up and walked to the bathroom to rinse his face. When he walked back toward the living room, he passed The Wall. It had been Martha's idea. From 1967 until late 1997 — five years after Martha's cancer overtook their lives — she had taken a picture of the Arlington Senators high school basketball team, had it framed, and hung it on the wall that led from their living room to their bedrooms. Thirty pictures in three neat columns, each representing a decade, capped off by five consecutive state championships starting in 1992, the very year after Martha had died. Jack had continued Martha's tradition by framing a picture each year after her death. The Wall was a shrine of sorts, of Jack's tenure as head coach of the Senators. No one was as great a coach as Jack Dempsey, Martha reminded her shy, humble husband, who had initially objected to The Wall when he saw the very first team picture she'd hung.

When he returned to the living room, the Coach reached for his keys and was just about to head out to Hank's Diner for his mid-morning cup of coffee and discussion with the gathering of eagles, a couple of his old buddies, now all retired. When he reached for the door, the phone rang. The now infrequent sound startled him at first, but then he headed for the relic of a white corded phone on the kitchen wall.

"Coach Dempsey, this is Carlos Lopez."

The memory wheels turned to reverse, then fast-forward in the Coach's mind, which had slowed a bit over the years. "Carlos?"

"Class of '95 Senators, point guard."

A pause and then he remembered. "Hey, Carlos, how are you? Wow, forgive my slowing gears. How the heck are you?"

"Great, Coach. How are you?"

Coach hesitated for a second, "Fine, just fine."

The two talked for another minute. Then Carlos asked, "Coach, can we meet for dinner one night? I'd love to catch up and also to run something by you."

"Well, sure, I guess that would be kinda fun."

The two came up with a date—the following week on Wednesday night.

~

After he hung up the phone, the Coach made his way to Hank's Diner in a local strip mall. Hank Milton had stayed in business now for more than thirty years, hanging on to the restaurant even now mainly because of a flock of old-timers like Jack.

Already seated at the counter, Wally Sanders turned his shaved, gleaming head toward the door when he heard its faint squeak, still there despite Hank's valiant efforts with WD-40 lubricant spray.

"Well, here's the liberal senator from the great state of Virginia now!"

Coach just nodded to deflect the jab. He did not look at Wally but at Hank and said, "Sir, a coffee for me and a sock for my friend's mouth!"

All three men laughed and converged at the corner of the counter. Each morning, they all discussed the daily news in a manner that was halfway between "The Daily Show" with John Stewart and "Meet the Press."

"So, I checked my 401K the other day, and I'm happy to say that I still have enough money for a cup of coffee here and an occasional doughnut," said the Coach as he motioned to Hank for a frosted doughnut, his usual. "Thank God for the fiscal genius of the Republicans."

"Tax and spend Democrat!" Wally said.

"Now, boys, let's play nice."

"It's the damned liberal media that will do us all in," Wally said, reaching for his cup of coffee. "Now they're harping on just allowing all those illegal aliens amnesty. Let them all pay taxes like me, then we'll talk amnesty, amigo!"

"You mean the same liberal media who got us out of Vietnam."

"Don't get me started on Vietnam, Coach," Wally said.

Chapter 3
Put Me in the Game

By the time Roger and Mary had arrived at the office, Janice had broken the news to the entire company, before Jim Talon had a chance to send his e-mail. *And so it begins,* Carlos thought to himself as the calls began to flood in from people who were the idle curious. Roger had already stopped in and congratulated Carlos but could not resist offering to mentor him if he ever needed help getting his "sea legs." Carlos gritted his teeth and thanked Roger for his generous, albeit arrogant, offer.

While Carlos was fielding phone messages about his promotion, thanks to Janice's premature news release, he noticed Mary walking into the office at 10:15 A.M., well over an hour late. She dropped her bag on her desk, took off her coat, and headed straight to the kitchen for her morning cup of coffee. Carlos started to get out of his chair but held himself back. Instead, he continued listening to phone messages, making notes, and thinking.

About a half hour later, Mary strolled into Carlos' new office, put her mug on his desk, and plopped down in a chair. "Well, now you're the man!"

Carlos was a bit distracted and had only caught the last few words. "Huh?" he asked, looking up at Mary smiling at him.

"You're the commandant...*el heffe*...the supreme commander. You're large and in charge," she said, winking and guzzling a swig of her coffee, holding the cup with both hands.

"I'm not sure I'd put it that way."

"Tell me you haven't wanted this office."

"Not really."

Mary almost spit out her coffee but covered her mouth instead to prevent spraying the desktop, then reached for a tissue on the far side of Carlos' desk. "Oh, come on!" she said, after she regained her composure.

Carlos could feel his temperature starting to rise and the hair on the back of his neck tingle. "Look Mary, first, no, I have not wanted this office. Second, tomorrow when you come to work, please get in on time, and... ." He stopped short of telling her she was an insinuating, insolent little twit.

"Well, tell me how you really feel, el supremo."

"You wouldn't like it," he blurted and then regretted having let Mary get to him so quickly.

"I can handle it," she said standing.

"Later," he stood up and towered over her. "Now it's time for you to stop drinking coffee and to get to work."

With that she pivoted and walked away. "Screw you," she said, under her breath.

"Mary, hold it right there. What did you say?"

She turned around, her face beet red, looking like she could eat the head off a chicken and said, "Nothing."

"I thought...," Carlos began to say but clipped the sentence. "We'll talk later."

"Right," she said and spun around so fast that she spilled coffee on the floor. She looked at the spot and kept walking out the door.

Now that went well, Carlos thought to himself. Less than two hours into his new leadership role and every one of his team had given him a genuine pain in the neck. And his day was just beginning. About thirty minutes later, Jim Talon walked into Carlos' new office waving an e-mail he'd gotten from one of the consultants in the field, a note sent from Janice about Carlos' new promotion. "What the hell is this?" Jim said, slamming the unofficial announcement on Carlos' desk.

Carlos read it, blushed, and said, "Janice is at it again."

"Well, stop her. She's been a gossip hound forever."

"What was George's approach?"

"It's your turn now. George is gone. Rein in that big-mouth gossip and do it fast. Take charge, for God's sake!" With that Jim crumpled up the paper and threw it at the basket, missing it by several feet, and stormed out.

~

Later that morning, Janice sat in Carlos' office smiling—at first. "Well, how's the first day at the helm?" She said it almost like she was his first mate.

"I've had better days."

"I'm surprised. Would have thought this day would be starred in your diary."

"Janice, we need to chat. Jim was just in my office," Carlos said, nearly choking as he said the "my office" part. "He wasn't happy."

"Really?"

"Yes. He had a note from a field guy who already knew about my promotion before Jim had time to announce it, as planned, by e-mail this morning."

"And?"

"And, he was upset...very upset."

"Why?"

"Because you released the news before him."

"He was angry with me?"

"Yes, with good reason, I think."

"How so, Carlos?"

"Look, you have to stop gossiping. It's hurting you, and frankly me, now that I'm your supervisor."

"Boy, you did drink the Kool-Aid."

"Janice, please, I'm trying to help you."

"Right!"

"Jim isn't happy, and neither am I."

"So, exactly what do you want me to do when I hear information?"

"Keep it to yourself, for starters."

"And whatever happened to the Constitution and free speech?"

"Janice, you're reaching now. I just want you to understand…."

Janice cut him off, "Are we finished here?"

"Well, for now, I guess."

With that she got up and left the office as fast as her feet could carry her straight back to her e-mail.

Chapter 4
Dinner with the Coach

Tony's Italian Restaurant, a small place in North Arlington, bustled with a full house of customers and a number of other people waiting. Waiters and busboys whizzed by at breakneck speed. Carlos was about ten minutes early, but the Coach was already seated in the booth. As soon as the Coach saw Carlos being escorted to the table, he got up, grabbed Carlos' hand, and pulled him in for a man-bump hug.

"Carlos, great to see you, son." Looking at Carlos, the Coach said, "Wow. Either you've grown, or I've shrunk!"

Carlos laughed."Coach, man, you look great."

With that, they sat down and started to catch up, with their laughter free flowing. Throughout the course of the meal, the topic of the Coach's wife came up, as did his retirement. They also discussed Carlos's graduation from college, his career, and especially his new promotion.

"Wow, you're pretty young to be a manager. Congratulations, Carlos."

"Or condolences."

"How so?" asked the Coach.

Carlos described his old boss, George Hampton, who had occupied the office for so many years. George had become an institution at JTS and in the consulting world. Carlos had learned a lot from George and became his protégé. Life had been great for Carlos, including working on a team for such a sure-footed leader as George. Then, George retired, and Carlos got tapped on the shoulder by Jim Tallon. "I was honored, " Carlos said, "don't get me wrong, but it's really scary, you know?"

The Coach listened as he had always done, leaning forward, looking straight at Carlos, not making a sound, and nodding as Carlos described his first day on the job, in his new office. Everything that could have gone wrong did. "I felt like the whole promotion was snakebit, right from the get-go."

Again, the Coach just listened.

Then Carlos started to talk about all the things he didn't know, how he wasn't certain that he was ready for the job. His education had not been as rigorous, his experience not deep enough. "Maybe I need to take a step back, not take this thing on right now until I'm better prepared," he said. And then his voice of doubt trailed off into silence. The coach looked at him, saying nothing, just looking.

After thirty seconds, Carlos broke the silence. "Coach, what do you think?"

The coach reached for his glass of water, swallowed as if he were preparing for a speech, put it down, collected his thoughts, and said, "Carlos, I don't know anything about your business. So, may I ask a few questions?"

"Sure."

"Do you respect your current boss—Jim Talon?"

"Yes."

"Do you consider him experienced in your business?"

"Sure, Jim's the founder of our business and a guru in the field."

"How about his judgment? Does he make pretty sound decisions?"

"Jim's one of the smartest, most deliberative guys I've ever met."

"OK, so then why do you think he decided to promote you and not any number of other people in your company?"

Carlos stared at the Coach, then at the table, then back at the Coach, and said, "I...I'm not sure."

"I think I know," the Coach said, reaching for another sip of his water.

Chapter 5
In Foul Trouble

A week later, the first disturbing e-mail came from Wally, his long-time buddy from the diner. The Coach opened it. It was a picture of a crowded downtown with every store having a mock Hispanic name, like Jalapeño Heaven Restaurant, Juan's Gas Hacienda, and such. The downtown was littered with empty tequila bottles, cars on blocks, and guys sleeping under sombreros. The sign above the picture said, "America… Home of the Brave and Land of the Illegal Aliens."

A shy man, the Coach could feel his face getting hot. He had suffered from blushing since he was a kid. Whenever he became embarrassed or angry, the blood lit up his face like a Christmas tree. Today, his cheeks were beet red. He had known that Wally had been a political conservative, and though against illegal immigrants, he was fair. While he'd spoken out vehemently about illegal immigration, he'd never crossed the line into racism. So, the Coach had debated how to handle his coffee time with Wally when next they met at Hank's.

The second disturbing e-mail from Wally came about three days after the Coach had decided not to say anything and just let the first e-mail slip into oblivion. This one was captioned "A Few Good Illegals!" The picture showed several Hispanic men swimming across the Rio Grande with Marine Corps recruiters on the other side, greeting them. In the next frame, the illegals were in combat uniforms and heading across a bridge to Afghanistan. "Damn it, Wally, that's it!" he yelled to his computer screen, and almost simultaneously he turned beet red.

The Coach did not sleep well that night, just thinking of how he might approach Wally the next day. He'd considered several options and decided on sending Wally a reply to his original e-mail:

Wally,

Please remove me from your mailing list of any further e-mails about illegal immigrants.

Jack

P.S.: See you tomorrow at Hank's

The next day, the Coach made it to Hank's about a half hour later than usual, only to find Hank with a couple of other customers. The Coach made his way to the end of the counter, where the three men had gathered for many years. Hank eventually wandered down to where the Coach sat.

"Hey, where's Wally? He already come and go?" asked the Coach, extending his coffee cup for a refill.

"Wally didn't come today. And he won't be coming any time soon, I'd guess."

"What's wrong?"

"He's just pissed at you."

The Coach began to get red again and said, "He's pissed at me? Did you see the two e-mails he sent to me about immigrants? WAY off base, Hank. Way off."

"I didn't see them, but he claims they were just jokes — nothing malicious."

Fortunately, the Coach anticipated such a "boys-will-be-boys" approach defense from Hank, so he slapped down printouts of both jokes on the counter, like a prosecutor offering stark, visual evidence to the jury. Hank looked at the pictures, cleared his throat and said, "Wally was just pissed about all the changes going on…you know how traditional he is."

"I do. But that's no excuse for this kind of stuff. Come on."

"No, I agree. Just cut him a little slack."

"Hey, I'm here. He's not."

Later that evening the Coach got his one-line response from Wally:

> *The hell with you! And don't send me any e-mails either.*

The Coach got red in the face and then deleted the e-mail.

Chapter 6
A Head Fake

The phone call came in about 4:30 P.M. "This is Carlos Lopez."

"Are you the supervisor of Janice Rollins?"

"Yes," Carlos said, thinking how strange that sounded to him—being a supervisor.

The voice on the other end of the line was that of the CEO from a client company. This CEO had asked JTS to conduct a climate survey that included personal, anonymous interviews, and Janice had been assigned to the project. According to the CEO's version of the story, Janice had said in the course of her interviews that she'd heard some bad stuff about the CEO, and so had asked a particular interviewee to be as candid as possible. Unknown to Janice, the person she'd said this to was the CEO's daughter, who had a different last name by marriage. The daughter reported this conversation to her father—and now her father was on the call with Carlos. Not only would he fire JTS, he was likely going to sue the company for defamation. Then he hung up.

Carlos just sat—stunned, then angry. He picked up the phone and called Janice, who was joking and talking with Mary and Roger in the common area near her cubicle. "Yeah, Carlos, what do you need?"

"Please come to my office, now" he said, slamming the phone down.

When Janice made it to the door, she quipped, "A bit testy, aren't we?"

"Just shut the door."

By the time she sat down, she said, "What's going on?"

"I'll tell you what's going on, your gossip may get us into a lawsuit. That's what's going on, Janice!"

"Wow, Carlos, what planet are you on? You're acting like a real jerk!"

That's when he lost his temper and recounted the story that the CEO had told him…punctuated with references to her loud mouth, her gossiping, and her genuine nosiness. And every time she started to speak, Carlos cut her off. Finally, he told her he didn't want to hear her gossiping anymore. Period. And, he wanted her to write up her response in detail before he spoke to Jim Talon and their corporate counsel. Then he dismissed her summarily, "Get that memo to me by 8 A.M. sharp tomorrow."

Shaking and disoriented, Janice almost knocked over the chair as she stood up. If it weren't so serious a situation, her awkwardness could have been funny. But there were no smiles to be had by either of them.

That evening, Carlos fumed into the night and slept fitfully. The next morning, when he greeted Jim Talon, Jim asked Carlos to step into his office. He pulled off his reading glasses and looked up from *The Wall Street Journal*. "I got a call from Janice last night." Carlos turned red and gripped the arms of the chair. Carlos thought: *That big mouth had not only gotten them into a lawsuit, but she'd also done an end run to my boss…to embarrass me even further.* As far as Carlos was concerned, she'd just declared war.

"She called you?"

"She's pretty pissed."

"She's pissed. Did she tell you that one of our new clients not only fired us but also may well be suing us because of her big mouth?"

"Let's start with the facts here," Jim said.

With that he launched into a withering series of questions, requiring only a yes or no from the defendant, or so Carlos felt.

No—he had not asked her side of the story.

Yes—he did call her a gossip.

No—he did not let her talk because when she did, she was disrespectful and rude.

Yes—he did suppose he had intimidated, even insulted her.

Yes—he was very angry.

When that line of fact-finding questioning was over, Jim told Carlos what Janice had told him last night and what was in her memo, to be delivered this morning along with her resignation. Some research by Jim had revealed that the CEO's daughter has a more than serious case of paranoia. It was the CEO's daughter who had told Janice that she had heard that a lot of dirt was coming out from these interviews. Janice had remained neutral. She'd been doing these interviews for years. When Janice left, she had a sense that this woman would be a problem and mentioned it to Roger, prior to Carlos having called her into his office. But she had never gotten the opportunity to defend herself and he, Carlos, had only assumed that because she was a gossip in the office, she was the same in the field — which, in Jim's experience, was not true.

"But you told me to rein her gossiping in. Remember?"

"I did. But not to treat her unfairly."

"But I…"

"Look, Carlos, we can't afford to lose Janice. She's a strategic genius. Sometimes, a gossiping pain in the rear. But she's worth a little discomfort for the long haul. We need to keep her. We need to fix this thing, ASAP. In fact, I want to see both of you in my office today, at 8:30. I'll facilitate this thing between you two—but don't let this happen again. I'm very disappointed."

So was Carlos. Disappointed, confused, and angry.

~

The facilitated session with Jim had more than its share of awkward moments. When Carlos entered the room, Jim was seated across the table from Janice, and he motioned Carlos to sit beside her. Jim began by announcing why they were all there—to help discuss what had happened and figure out a way to go forward without repeating such behavior in the future.

The ground rules: Carlos and Janice were only to answer Jim's questions, and answer to him directly. No cross-talk at this point. Jim asked Janice to go first. She recounted the situation just as Jim had explained it earlier to Carlos. Then Carlos spoke. He told the story from his perspective—Janice had frequently been a gossip, and he assumed in this case that such loose talk again had caused the problem, so he felt compelled to act in order to save the account and blunt the possible lawsuit.

Jim nodded and said, "OK, we have the facts on the table. Now how do you both feel about what has happened?"

Again, Jim turned to Janice first. "I feel like I was the victim of innuendo and unfairly treated," she said, looking only at Jim.

Jim nodded and turned to Carlos, who said, "I'm embarrassed and angry at the same time."

"Can you explain?" Jim asked.

"Yes. I jumped the gun on this, I admit that, based on my assumption that Janice was a gossip."

Janice started to say something, but Jim held up his hand like a stop sign, and Janice leaned back into her chair.

"So, do you think it is fair to say that you assumed Janice had said something to the CEO's daughter—based on her previous behavior?"

"Yes."

"So what has made you angry?"

"You really want me to tell you?"

"Of course, that's why we're here."

"OK. Two reasons. First, I was still angry that Janice announced my promotion prematurely."

"And?"

"This revolves around a conversation you and I had. Do you want me to still go forward?"

Jim looked at Carlos and then at Janice, searching his mind. "Sure. Go ahead."

"When I got promoted and after Janice released the info, you told me to rein her gossiping in. Those were the specific words you said."

Janice shot a look at Jim that had daggers in it.

"Well, yes, I indicated that you were now a manager... and...I..."

"Hey, just a second," Carlos said, "I thought we were being honest here." You specifically told me, and I quote, 'George is gone. Rein that gossip in and do it fast. Take charge, for God's sake!'"

Jim's face blanched as he heard the very words he'd told Carlos following Janice's leaking the announcement of Carlos' promotion to the entire firm. "Well, I'm not sure those were the exact words but..."

"They were the exact words."

"Well, the point is we have to all be open and honest with each other, so I'll take you at your word, Carlos," Jim said. Now he was blushing.

"OK."

Jim said he accepted that both Carlos and Janice had a legitimate right to feel the way they did. Then he asked them about how they could restore their relationship. What would it take?

"I'm not sure," said Janice, "Several companies have offered me more money. Maybe it's time for me to move on."

"So, are you saying that, even if we accept that Carlos made a mistake based on previous experience when you prematurely released information about his promotion, there is no hope for reconciliation here?"

They went back and forth. Jim continued to ask Carlos and Janice what it might take to reconcile their differences. With no immediate resolution, both of them agreed to think about the situation and discuss it early the next week.

Chapter 7
Taking a Time Out

At Carlos' request, the Coach again met him for dinner at Tony's Italian Restaurant. This time Carlos arrived fifteen minutes before the Coach. After they both had ordered, Carlos explained the entire incident that he'd had with Janice and the facilitation session that Jim had conducted afterward. The Coach listened intensely while he watched Carlos. He never said a word—just listened. Finally, when Carlos ran out of words, he asked the Coach, "So, now what do you think?"

"That you're working through a bump in the road."

"A bump in the road? That's it?"

"I'd say."

"Coach, can you give me a little more guidance here?"

"OK. If you want my ten-second leadership lecture."

"Shoot."

"A good leader has to stay balanced. Three things help you stay balanced: Good Character, Good Sense, and Good Will. That's it."

Carlos laughed and said, "I'm not sure you used all ten seconds on that one! Can you go into a little more detail?"

"OK. Let me tell you a story." And with that the Coach told Carlos the story of Lenny Jacobson, the captain of the first Senators team he ever coached. Lenny was a kind of golden boy. He'd been elected captain of the team before the Coach was brought in mid-season to take over for the regular coach, who had moved out of town due to a family crisis. Lenny was a showboat, and Carlos knew how much the Coach disliked show-offs. So the Coach and

Lenny locked horns almost immediately. The two pushed each other's buttons, and a vicious cycle of distrust and anger hurt their relationship.

Then, Lenny decided to shut down the team. He slowed the game with a lack of enthusiasm and hustle, which, coming from a point guard, is death to any team. So the Coach replaced him; however, the back-up point guard, Lenny's replacement, looked to Lenny on the bench for hints about how he should act. It was as if Lenny were coaching the team, not the Coach.

After losing four games straight, the Coach asked to meet with Lenny. "It was the toughest thing I ever did, admitting to a seventeen-year-old kid that I needed his help to win."

"I'd want to boot him off the team," Carlos said as he reached for his water.

"Don't think I didn't consider that option, but I feared the rest of the team would go with him!"

"So, what happened?"

"I decided that it was my job to establish trust with Lenny. That's when I figured out The Trust Triangle, something I learned in a communications class as an undergraduate."

"The Trust Triangle. OK, I'll bite. What is that?"

The Coach explained that Aristotle, the ancient Greek philosopher, had come up with three critical attributes that speakers must demonstrate to establish their trustworthiness: Good Character, Good Sense, and Good Will. Each of these three "legs" comprise The Trust Triangle. Each was vital and required to make trust between two people work—whether that individual was speaking to a crowd or connecting on a one-to-one, personal level.

"So when it came to Lenny, I started at the very base of the triangle. I used the five C's of Good Character:

Candor, Communication, Commitment, Consistency, and Courage."

"Can you give me the details on the five C's?"

With that, the Coach, in between bites of his lasagna, outlined the five C's.

First, he explained that good character requires what the Coach called candor—complete honesty. You must be completely clear and honest—the base line for any credibility you will ever have. Clarity and honesty in the face of difficult circumstances really count. "Sometimes you have to swallow your ego—in fact most times—to be completely honest."

"Like when you negotiated with Lenny over control of the team."

"Yep, tough stuff, but if you care enough about the team or the principle at stake, you do it. But that's only half of the deal."

"OK, what's the rest of the story?"

"Candor respects the other person's ego. Let's take Janice, for example. Sounds like a smart woman who's got some reason or need to engage in gossip. Now, I'm no psychologist, but I'm guessing that's a need she's had for most of her life and unless she goes to therapy, you won't be changing that too fast."

Carlos nodded "yes" emphatically.

"So, you'll have to consider her ability, maybe even a pretty fragile ego, when you tell her 'the truth' about herself. Maybe talk to her about how the gossip affects you, less about her gossip problem…more about its effect on other people, like you."

With that last comment, Carlos took a blue 3" × 5" spiral notebook out of his pocket, and he began to take notes.

The coach smiled. It was exactly the same kind of notebook he had used for years to make his coaching notes. Even in practice, the Coach always had the note-book with him in his warm-up suit.

Carlos caught the Coach's smile and smiled back as if to say, *Yep, I really learned a lot from your coaching.* Then, he said, "Good, Coach, go on please."

"Next is Communication," said the Coach, "which sounds like a touchy-feely term. Let me tell you how hard it is for so many leaders to let others know what they're thinking. Remember, in the face of no communication, people will make up stories. That's exactly how gossip and rumor work."

When Carlos heard that comment about gossip, a huge light bulb went off in his head. "So, Janice might be so starved for information that she makes it up?"

"Maybe. As a leader, the more you communicate with everyone on your team, the less there is for people to have to make up to fill the void."

Carlos jotted more notes in his blue notebook.

Then, Coach talked about commitment and consistency together. "People just want to know that you're in it for the long haul—committed. If they think you're just tagging the corporate base to move on to the next big job, it's pretty unlikely they will invest in you."

"Invest?"

"Yes, invest their time, attention, and energy. That's all they have...their only currency. And whenever people believe that a leader is just a flash in the pan, they're careful about wasting their personal resources on that person."

"OK."

"One more thing. Consistency means doing what you say you'll do. In a sense, it's about integrity...staying consistent to yourself and your word. In fact, all reputation comes from how others view your consistency."

"Really?"

The Coach explained that all people could judge was what you did. And when that was always consistent, they saw you as a person of integrity (authentic) and dependable. When people see that they can trust your responses to be consistent, they'll trust you.

"Makes sense," Carlos said after the Coach paused to take a sip of water. "What about consistency?"

"In coaching, there's a thing I call consistent individuality." The Coach described his relationship to Lenny. "Look, I had to be consistent on most things. Everyone had to practice, and if they missed practice, they could NOT start the next game—no exceptions, except a death in the family or something like that. That said, I had to treat each player as an individual. Remember how you needed tutoring in math?"

"Wow. I had forgotten that. You had the tutor come to practice, so I could be there but still get my tutoring. Haven't thought of that for years!"

"Every person is unique and has individual needs that have to be met within the context of the entire team—consistent individuality. It's like when you go into Starbucks for coffee. All the customers want some form of caffeine but each wants it differently. One person just wants black coffee, another a latte, and still someone else wants a frappuccino."

Finally, the Coach explained how it took Courage to speak out when things weren't going well, or even if they were going fine, but needed to be even better. Again, the conversation with Lenny took guts (courage), and ego subordination, for the Coach to be successful. Candor isn't easy and demands courage. Suddenly, the Coach's mind flashed up a picture of his e-mail to Wally Sanders about the illegal immigration jokes. Now he wondered if he'd ever see Wally again. "Courage is doing what's right, even when it means losing something or someone important to you, to keep something even more important—self-respect."

Again, Carlos wrote some notes.

"Wow. That's good," Carlos said, sipping his coffee as he continued to write in his spiral binder.

Good Character (The Five C's)

1. **Candor:** Swallow your ego and tell the truth. Others have needs. Consider their egos and be honest.

2. **Communication:** People need information or they make it up—gossip.

3. **Commitment:** People will offer their personal investment—time, attention, and energy—if they believe you'll be around for the long haul. And, do what you say you'll do—always.

4. **Consistency:** Consistent individuality—leaders need not only to be consistent with the team but also allow for individual needs of each team member.

5. **Courage:** Speak out when it's the right thing to do. It's almost never easy. Respect yourself and others.

The Trust Triangle

TRUST:
Good Character

1. Candor
2. Communication
3. Commitment
4. Consistency
5. Courage

TRUST

Good Character

Chapter 8
A Protest Call

Rehearsing what he might say, the Coach drove up the tree-lined street slowly. It was early morning. The white colonial house with the green shutters was announced by a perfectly manicured lawn—something that had always been a source of pride for Wally. Ironically, the Coach noticed a real estate sign about five doors down that read "Foreclosure Sale."

The Coach knew that every morning, Wally went on a two-mile walk at 7:30 A.M. Today was no exception. Like clockwork, Wally's front door opened, and he stepped out dressed in his blue warm-up suit and dark knit stocking hat and gloves. When he started down the driveway, the Coach got out of his car and approached the bottom of the driveway to intercept Wally.

When he reached the sidewalk, Wally was startled to hear the Coach call out his name.

"Damn!" Wally yipped.

"Didn't mean to scare you."

"You don't scare me, Coach."

"I didn't mean it that way, Wally. We need to talk."

"I don't think so. It's pretty clear that you think I'm a racist. And you're some sort of saint."

Wally was walking at full tilt by this time, and frankly the Coach was out of shape and out of breath. So he grabbed Wally by the arm, "Come on Wally, you win. OK. I can't stay with you. You happy now?"

Wally did flash a small, quick smile. "Times change, eh Coach?"

"Yeah, they do," the Coach said, bending over to breathe a bit better. "I'm in sorry shape."

That was just enough humility for Wally. "OK, let's slow it down."

"Thanks."

And with that the two men got into sync. The Coach explained that he wanted to figure out what happened. He knew that Wally, a retired police officer, was a straight-up guy, who had always been fair and evenhanded with everyone he'd ever come in contact with—good guys and bad guys alike. Wally took this all in with a relaxed look on his face.

"Look, I know we're on opposite sides in this immigration issue."

"You've got that right."

"But you've always been a fair, decent guy. That's why when I got those two racial e-mails forwarded to me from you, I thought about how out of character it was for you."

Wally just slowly nodded.

"So, I'm just trying to understand what was going on. How did you come to send them?"

Wally looked more than a bit uncomfortable. There was a long silence and then he spoke at first slowly, "You know Eleanor?"

"Yes, you've been dating her for a couple of months."

"Had been dating her," Wally corrected their status.

"What happened?"

"I thought we both saw eye to eye on illegal immigration. If something's illegal...then it's, well...illegal. That's how I feel."

"OK. I get that."

"Yeah, but Eleanor started saying things...racial stuff. At first I laughed and shrugged them off. You know. Then she started sending jokes around and telling me to forward them to friends—spread the word kind of thing. That's how you got the jokes. I was in a rush one day and just started forwarding them. I know it's dumb. No excuse. I think you caught me being duped and then ashamed. I overreacted—embarrassed."

The Coach listened.

"One day after you sent your note and after my reply, she sent me a few more to pass on. This time I read each one carefully and was shocked. I wouldn't send them to Adolf Hitler!"

The Coach laughed.

"They were racist trash. All of a sudden my blinders were off, and I could see now. That's when we broke up—last week."

"I'm sorry. I know that you really liked her," the Coach said softly.

"Not enough to put up with that stuff," Wally said, stopping. "I'm really sorry, Coach."

The Coach stuck out his hand, "You're a good friend, Wally. Anyway, who would I fight with over politics if I didn't have you?"

"Got a point," he said, "good point."

Chapter 9
Setting the Record Straight

Janice had taken off the couple of days following the session with Jim Talon. When she returned to work, Carlos asked if she could meet with him in his office later in the day. She came in to see him at about 4 P.M.

"You want to sit down?"

"I'm fine," she said, her arms tightly hugging her body.

"Well, I'd like to start by apologizing," Carlos said with a strain in his voice. "I reacted — I overreacted — without getting all the facts first. Mostly, I'm upset because I didn't give you the benefit of the doubt. I'm sorry for how I acted and wanted to let you know."

She didn't say anything, but she released the tight bear hug on herself.

Carlos filled the gap. "Look, I don't expect you to forgive me now. I'll work at repairing our relationship."

"OK," Janice said. She turned around and left the office.

After everyone had left that night, Carlos walked into Jim Talon's office and told him what had happened.

"That's it?" Jim asked.

"What do you mean?"

"She ended the meeting?"

"I guess so; really there was nothing left to talk about."

"Yeah, but as the boss, you decide when a meeting is over."

"I, ah…. Well, I thought it went well."

"You've got a lot to learn about being in charge, Carlos."

As Jim spoke, Carlos' eyes drifted over Jim's shoulder to the picture on the wall, the one of the Marines planting the flag at Iwo Jima. He wondered what it had been like for those guys.

"Carlos, you with me on this, son?" Jim said when he noticed that Carlos had tuned out.

"Yes, sure. Take charge. But I didn't want to throw salt into the wound."

"I hear you but remember who's the boss—you are."

When he left the meeting with Jim, Carlos was thoroughly confused. He should take charge but not make Janice mad was the message rattling through his brain. Be hard and soft at the same time....kind of a mixed message, he thought.

The next morning Carlos arrived at the office at 7:00. He e-mailed the team, notifying them that he'd decided to have a staff meeting, at 9 A.M., to talk about expectations for the team for the year. Jim had told him to begin formulating a revenue strategy that would succeed in spite of the down market. In short, how could they not only make but also exceed their budget as they had for the last fifteen years?

Janice said she couldn't make it until 9:30. Roger had decided to take a day off and sent a reply to Carlos's e-mail announcing his unilateral decision, and Mary didn't come in until ten. Carlos, fuming, called off the meeting and reset it for the next day instead, telling everyone it was mandatory.

~

Janice was seated in the conference room and Roger came in a little past nine, but Mary was absent. Carlos conducted the meeting anyway. He felt stiff. His speech seemed like a monologue. Neither Janice nor Roger took a single note as Carlos talked about budget predictions and models for increased marketing. He was wrapping up when Mary came in, still wearing her hat and gloves, and sat down.

"That's it for now. I'll let you know when the next meeting will be in advance," he said and then added, "Mary, please hold for a minute."

"I haven't even had time for my coffee."

"It will have to wait."

Janice's eyebrows rose as she looked at Roger. They slowly got up and left.

When both had exited the room, Carlos said, "Why were you late for the staff meeting?"

"I missed my bus."

"Don't miss it again."

"Yes, SIR!" she said with a sarcastic, almost teen-aged tone that would try the patience of even an experienced parent.

"And, Mary, lose the attitude."

"What ATTITUDE, Carlos?"

"The one you're using right now."

"How about YOUR attitude. All I'M IN CHARGE!"

"That's it, Mary, I'm suspending you for a day to cool it."

"Not before I talk to Jim."

"Do that from your home phone. I want you gone for the day."

"You're a jerk."

"Before you get yourself fired, I strongly suggest you leave for the day."

"No need, Adolf, I quit!" she said, pushing back her chair with enough force to topple it. She stepped around the chair and left the room, not before slamming the door.

Carlos composed himself and headed right for Jim's office only to find Mary crying with her head on Jim's desk and Jim patting her hand. Having been preempted, Carlos walked back to his office and waited for Jim's inevitable phone call. It came about ten minutes later. Both angry and confused about how the heck he should have, could have, led such a crew of folks, Carlos entered Jim's office, shut the door, and sat in the chair facing Jim's desk.

"Carlos, I just spoke to Mary, who told me that you fired her."

"That's nuts. I told her to go home for the day."

"Because she was a few minutes late for an ad hoc meeting."

"Is that what she told you?"

"So, why don't you tell me?"

"She was forty-five minutes late for a meeting I told her about two days ago."

"Nevertheless, suspension? Come on, Carlos."

"I suspended her for her attitude."

"How the hell do you measure that?"

Carlos could feel his face getting beet red, which upset him even more than Jim's approach.

"Carlos, you have to take charge without destroying your team."

Carlos bit his tongue, rather than tell Jim what he was really thinking, which was: Why did I ever agree to take this promotion?

Chapter 10
Back in the Game

Two days following Mary's suspension, Carlos was sitting in his office when Mary came in—late but only by a minute or two. She glared at Carlos and sat down. He could actually feel the anger radiating from her.

He'd thought all weekend about what he would say. At times when he rehearsed what he might say to Mary, some words were angry, others less so, and still others registered disappointment. Then, despite his own feelings of anger, he remembered what the Coach had said about the five C's. He remembered the Coach's words and took a leap of faith.

"I'm sorry that our new relationship has started off so rocky."

She didn't move a muscle, just looked straight at him.

"OK. Then I need to ask you a question," he said slowly. "Is there some reason in your personal life why you're so late, so often?"

"My personal life is none of your business."

"You're right. Your personal life isn't my business. However, it's impacting your work life, and that is my area of interest. I just thought if I could understand—"

She'd cut him off. "There's nothing to understand. I'll work it out myself," she said, as her voice broke and a tear rolled down her right cheek.

Carlos remained silent.

"I'm just trying to balance so many things, my mother...," she stopped short and pulled back immediately as if she'd already said way too much to her new, young boss and former colleague.

Carlos waited to speak and then chose his words carefully. "You mentioned your mother — is she OK?"

"No, she is not," Mary blurted out. "She's very sick."

"Mary, I'm so sorry to hear that. Have you been taking care of her yourself?"

Mary could only nod her head while she wiped the stream of tears.

"I see. Can I assume that when you've come in later or left early, you were taking care of her?"

Again, a tearful nod from Mary.

"I'm sorry," he said. "Will you help me so we can figure out how to keep you taking care of your mother and allow you to be successful at work?"

When she nodded, Carlos took a deep breath and lightly pushed a box of tissues toward her.

The next day, Carlos had a staff meeting in the small conference room near his office. Janet, Roger, and even Mary were there promptly at 9:00 A.M. First, Carlos asked Mary to tell the group what was going on in her life. She had reluctantly agreed to discuss her mother's situation before this meeting — as she juggled her desire to get help against maintaining her privacy. Carlos explained that if the team were going to have to pick up the slack, they deserved some explanation.

She told the team that her mother had gotten sick and debilitated with congestive heart failure about a year ago, shortly after Mary joined the firm. Her mother had little money and no viable means of support, except for her social security and very small monthly dividends that had slowed to a trickle with the recession. So, Mary had rented out her mother's house to create income, taken her mother into her own two-bedroom apartment, and hired a health-care aide to care for her mother. The cost of the healthcare worker was more than significant, and the aide had trouble with the bus, her children, and her own convoluted life. Further, every weekend and evening Mary was the sole healthcare support—which wore her down. So, she was often late, had to leave work early, or was simply exhausted much of the time.

When she had finished, Carlos stood up and spoke. "I just found out about Mary's situation yesterday and wanted you all to know what was going on." He then proceeded to outline a proposal to allow Mary some much-needed flexibility. He noted that to make this work, everyone would have to agree to help out. Both Janice and Roger nodded. Carlos then suggested that Mary change her hours and come in routinely from ten to four and she could work from home for the other hours. She could telecommute one day a week to allow her the flexibility to accomplish things like shopping, paying bills, and all that needed tending to as she balanced this overwhelming schedule. Finally, Carlos said that the entire team would review the schedule of work every month to make sure it was working, but that he thought if he, Janice, and Roger pitched in for early morning briefings with clients, things could work.

Mary just stared at Carlos and then at her two teammates and began to cry. Carlos was not sure what to do but edged toward her and put a hand on her shoulder as she shuddered beneath his light touch. She did manage to say, "Thank you all. Thank you—so much."

Chapter 11
Huddle Up

It was Wednesday night again, and the Coach had agreed to meet with Carlos on the second and fourth Wednesdays of the month at Tony's Restaurant. In fact, Carlos began to think of this day as "Wednesdays with the Coach." This particular night, Carlos actually met the Coach in the parking lot, and they walked in together. By now, the hostess knew them and the table that the two men preferred. So, without a word, other than "Good evening, gentlemen," she led them to their special table, a secluded booth in the rear of the dining room.

The two chatted about some of the local sports teams and the tough economy. When both topics had been wrung out, Carlos recounted Mary's situation. He also described his response: presenting the team with his proposal to support Mary during this difficult time by all pitching in, and their ready willingness to help out.

"Wow," the Coach said, "That's one of the best cases of honoring someone that I've heard in a while. Nice work."

"Honor—I never thought of it as that," said Carlos.

"Somewhat like respect—I just like honor more— takes it to a higher level for me."

"OK, I guess."

The Coach stopped there and explained that honor, for him, encompassed both caring and respect but was far more elevated. "Honor does two things. It exalts the other person being honored—and it humbles you in the process."

Carlos wrinkled his forehead at the Coach as if he'd just been asked to comment on some complex mathematics theorem.

The Coach caught the look and continued, "It's like when you get beaten by a better team in a big tournament. What do you do when the game is over?"

"You go home and sulk!"

The coach laughed and replied, "Before that!"

"Take a shower?"

"OK, rather than play a guessing game, right after you lose the game, it's on the losing coach and team to congratulate the winning team."

"Right, of course."

"That's a bit of the point here. In sports, honoring the winning team—respecting the winning team and humbling yourself at the same time—is built into the sports culture."

"I see. The act of honoring another allows you to be humbled, and that's a good thing?"

"Humility and honor help us all to revere another's talent and recognize our own strengths and challenges."

"I guess I understand congratulating when someone beats me…kind of. It's the second part, about humility, I'm not as clear about."

"There's an old saying, "'You don't have to blow out another's candle to make yours burn brightly.'"

"Ahhh. Giving an opponent the spotlight doesn't diminish what you do."

"In fact, it's the opposite. In life you get what you give. So when you give love, you get it back. When you give open and honest communication, that's what others will give back. And it works both ways—good and bad."

"Explain what you mean—both ways?"

"When you give something good, like you help someone move from their apartment to a new condo they just bought, what do they want to do for you?"

"Buy you a beer."

The Coach laughed. "Right, but don't they also expect that if you move and call them for help, that they'll help you?"

"Of course," answered Carlos as he reached for his water glass.

"Same thing happens when you harm someone. Maybe you put them down or shade the truth about them to hurt their reputation. What do they do when that happens?"

"Return the favor!"

"Yes, and that's called a vicious cycle. They do bad things to you and you turn around and reciprocate with another bad thing to them. Kind of how wars start."

"I can see that now."

"The reverse or virtuous cycle is also true. One good deed precipitates another—back and forth in a very positive loop," the Coach said, reaching for one of the hot rolls that the waiter had just brought.

"Never thought such a small word like honor had such a big impact in my life. Wow!"

"Yep. So, do you remember back when we talked about how good character had the five C's?"

With that, Carlos whipped out his notebook and read, "Candor, Communication, Commitment, Consistency, and Courage."

"Bingo! Well, just like the five C's, I have the five H's when it comes to Good Will....another piece of The Trust Triangle. In short, you have to honor or care about certain things to gain trust from others."

With his pen at the ready, Carlos said, "Shoot."

The Coach listed the five H's: Honor Yourself, Honor Other People, Honor the Company, Honor the Community, and Honor the Country and the World. He then began to talk about honoring yourself first. He told Carlos that all honor starts from the inside out. If a person doesn't honor himself or herself as special in the world—with definite strengths and definite challenges—honoring others is difficult, if not impossible. But once you're able to honor yourself, honoring others get easier.

"Yeah, but what does that look like? Honoring yourself?" Carlos asked.

"It's a lot like integrity. Sticking to the personal values you believe in, no matter how inconvenient the situation is. Like when going along with the group might be easier than doing what you know is right. Or, just doing the right thing—when maybe it isn't popular."

"Like the time you benched me in the finals for swearing at the referee? The fans didn't like that move at all."

It took a second or two for the Coach to react. "Yes, Carlos, I guess that's a good example," he said with a slight blush to his face. Then he cleared his throat and continued. "OK. So, honoring other people comes next as you expand your honor into the world. By honoring others—their values, worth and contributions—you teach yourself to be worthy of humility. You see, personal humility is like throwing a rock into a still lake. When the rock splashes, it sends out concentric circles that get larger and larger until the entire lake gets embraced by the circles."

"Amazing—I never thought of it that way," Carlos said.

"Honoring your company, your community, and your country all fall into line after that. Once you can honor yourself, then others, honoring the rest of the world gets easier every day."

"Wait a second, Coach," Carlos said. I'm not exactly sure about how honoring company, community, and country fit the other two…self and others."

The Coach explained to Carlos that people join a company because of its mission, vision and values—but leave because of bad bosses.

"The best people leave bad leaders because talented employees have options, and they exercise those options with their feet," the Coach said. "However, often before they leave the organization, angry employees begin to badmouth the place—the very place that had provided for them and their families." He told Carlos how such an attitude was poisonous to the company, and even more importantly, to the person spewing forth the venom. "My view is that if you don't like the place you work, change jobs. You'll be better off and so will your company." At the same time, the Coach pointed out that good leaders—the kind who have good character, good sense, and good-will—retained people, while bad leaders drove off the best and brightest, with a huge economic blow to the company. So, the message about honor applies to both leaders and their employees.

Community, the Coach explained, is the ecosystem where we live, work, and play. It's the system that sustains us and our families, and we all have an obligation to pay back to the community that has given us so much and sustains our existence.

"Simply put, Carlos, we're all obligated to give our time, talent and money to support and sustain the community that had been built by others for us. Sort of like standing on the shoulders of those who've come before us," the Coach said, reaching for his water. "That's why participating in local government, becoming a member of the local Lions, Kiwanis, or Chamber of Commerce, and generally taking a community leadership role show that you honor the place that gives you schools, safety, and much more."

Finally, the Coach explained, "Country and the World" is our ultimate responsibility to the wider good. The Coach sat up straighter in the booth and said, "The Constitution provides us all with a host of rights, unequaled anywhere in the world, and we owe it our service. Look, I know not everyone will want to go into the military, no matter how good I think it is for development of new leaders, but I do think every graduate of high school or college should spend two years in public service of some kind. I don't care whether it's teaching, emergency relief, or whatever—serving others with active, positive support."

The Coach spoke slowly and softly after hearing his own voice rise as he spoke about public service so passionately. "If you find a person stuck inside himself, only caring about himself or even just his family, that person gets landlocked."

"Landlocked, huh?" said Carlos.

"Too internally focused. We're pack animals. Social. We need to believe in something bigger than ourselves, or we start becoming way too myopic. Honor yourself, sure...but the further out you honor others, the company, the community and the country, the more you become a fully-realized person, in your own right."

The Coach went on to explain how honoring the world was a logical extension of honoring the country. Natural disasters like hurricanes, floods or earthquakes proved this point over and over. We're ALL part of a world, brothers and sisters, no matter what country we live in.

The two men talked nonstop throughout the meal as Carlos asked more and more questions about honor. Then the waiter came to clear the dishes, but before he could the Coach reached over and grabbed Carlos' empty plate and stacked it on his, then put on the butter plates and silver-ware—all in a neat pile for the waiter to take away more easily.

In fact, the waiter said, "Why thank you, sir, I appreciate it."

"And we really appreciated the great food and your service tonight."

After the waiter had taken away the dishes, Carlos winked at the Coach and said, "Honor."

The Coach winked back and said, "And now—dessert!"

With that, Carlos took out his blue spiral notebook and wrote in it.

Good Will

In his/her daily actions, good leaders:

1. Honor self by staying true to stated personal values.

2. Honor others' values, worth, and contributions.

3. Honor the company's mission, vision, and values.

4. Honor the community by giving time, talent, and money to it.

5. Honor the country and world by active, personal support.

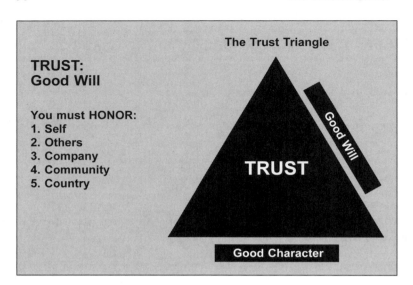

Chapter 12
The Secret Play

Another two weeks flew by in a flash. Both the Coach and Carlos had just ordered their usual meals at Tony's when Carlos noticed that the Coach was unusually quiet.

"Coach, everything alright?"

"Sure.. Fine," the Coach said, reaching for his water.

"Fine?"

The Coach nodded his head.

"I don't think so," Carlos shot back.

Slowly, the Coach lifted his head and looked directly at Carlos. Then he said, "Ten years ago today Emma died."

"Coach, I'm sorry."

"I should have known better than try to be good company tonight."

"If you want to talk about it…"

"Not sure. Just wanted to be honest with you."

"Look, I'd be honored to talk to you about it."

The Coach stirred his coffee more than he needed to, pulled out the spoon, and carefully placed it on his saucer. Then he stared into his still swirling coffee, as if he were in a trance. Carlos waited, quietly sitting there. Finally, the Coach looked up at Carlos and said, "I want to tell you a story — one I've never told anyone in my life."

Carlos felt a jolt of anticipation run up his spine. "Sure, Coach."

Drawing in a deep breath, the Coach began, "Emma was the love of my life."

Carlos saw him quickly wipe his right eye and then reach for his cup of coffee. After taking a sip, the Coach continued, "She was beautiful, smart, and as loving a person as I've ever met. So when she first got the diagnosis about her congestive heart failure, I was more devastated than she. Emma fought it for years, but that disease just wears you down physically and mentally. It's a slow death, but through it all, she remained the rock of our family."

Carlos just listened and nodded.

The Coach described her numerous treatments, surgeries, and hopeful new drugs, and finally her last few months as her spirit slowly left her body. The Coach had to stop several times to collect himself.

"I was with her all through the final months. I took a leave of absence from school. The faculty and the principal were very supportive," he said. "It was amazing. During those last few months Emma and I resolved the biggest failure of our marriage."

The Coach shifted in his seat as he prepared to tell the secret he and Emma had held for all those years. "When Emma and I were first married, we wanted to have children, but Emma couldn't get pregnant. Then about a year into our marriage, not long after Emma returned from a trip to see her mother on the West Coast, she announced to me that she no longer wanted to have children. I was shocked at her change of heart. Needless to say, I pumped her for what happened on the trip and why she'd changed her mind, but she refused to tell me. Just said she wanted to have her own career."

The Coach described the year following Emma's decision not to have children as the most difficult of their entire marriage, while he tried over and over to understand why she had suddenly not wanted children any longer. Later that year her mother died. Shortly after, Emma told the Coach that when she had visited her mother a year earlier, her mother knew she was dying and had told Emma that she had been adopted when she was one week old—a great shock to Emma. Further, her mother explained that Emma's parents were mixed races: her birth mother was white and Emma's father was African, from Nigeria. He had been an exchange student in graduate school and had met Emma's birth mother at Berkeley in San Francisco. They fell in love and Emma's birth mother got pregnant in her last year of graduate school. Emma's birth mother was unprepared to be a parent and gave her up for adoption.

Emma's mother had always wanted to tell Emma the story of her origins but put it off from year to year. However, when Emma told her mother that she was trying to have children, her dying mother knew she had to tell Emma the truth.

"Emma was devastated by the news, as you might imagine—more that she felt deceived and somehow unwanted—despite that her adoptive parents had raised her with such extraordinary love and affection. Nonetheless, she felt invalidated, even unworthy. That's the best way I can describe it."

"I'm so sorry for her and you, Coach. It must have been a very tough time for you."

"That year was the worst year of our marriage. When she finally told me the truth, Emma explained how during that long year she became obsessed by her personal feelings of confusion and invalidity."

The Coach described their marriage throughout that long year as Emma spiraled into depression. Finally, at the Coach's insistence, she went to counseling. A year after she started the counseling, Emma came out of her depression. However, she also announced that she would get a hysterectomy to ensure that she never had children.

At this point, the Coach broke down and Carlos reached over and put his hand on the Coach's arm. Finally, the Coach regained his composure and said, "I'm so sorry, Carlos, this is so unprofessional. I apologize."

"Coach, this had to be a very tough story to keep to yourself. And I feel honored that you told me."

"Thanks."

The Coach explained that because Emma never had children but knew that the Coach would have loved kids, she started The Wall—with all the team pictures—in their house in order to display all the Coach's "adopted sons."

Now, it was Carlos' turn to stare at the table in front of him.

"Carlos, you OK?" the Coach now asked him, in a quick role reversal.

"Fine."

"I don't think so."

Now it was Carlos stirring his coffee and staring deeply as the coffee swirled in his cup. "Coach, thanks for trusting me to hear your story," he said, pausing to collect his thoughts.

"I have a story, too."

"Are you ready to share it?"

"I don't think I'd ever be ready. But you're…well, I trust you."

"Thanks, Carlos."

Carlos began slowly, deliberately, "My mother brought me from Aruba to Miami. She gave a smuggler everything she had to bring us on a boat not fit to sail in a lake, let alone the ocean."

The coach remained silent but nodded as he listened to Carlos' story.

"My mother told me that my father had died when I was very young—had died trying to smuggle them out of Aruba. She had pictures and candles, a kind of shrine to him. She described him as a hero."

"You must have been proud."

"Until I found out the truth. When my mother was very ill with cancer, she told me that she needed to tell me the truth or she might be condemned by God. So one early afternoon in March, she told me what really happened," Carlos said, reaching for his coffee, as if to prepare his dry throat for his recitation.

"My mother told me the whole, ugly story. Early in my parents' marriage, my father worked in a factory in Aruba. He was hard working and smart, and he became a manager, but later he got a new boss, who he clashed with. Eventually he got fired and was unemployed for a very long time. After bouts with drinking and rage, he finally started to sell drugs to make money for the family."

The Coach just listened but tried not to react to the revelations that seemed very painful for Carlos.

"My mother was devastated by my father's new lifestyle. Eventually, she could not stand it so she escaped with what little money she could scrape together and came to America."

"Carlos, I'm so sorry. But didn't you say she brought you with her?"

"She did — inside her."

"She was pregnant?"

Carlos nodded.

"So when did your father find out he had a son?"

"Never."

The Coach looked him and said, "I don't understand."

Carlos took a long sip of his coffee, then cleared his throat and said, "My mother never told him."

The silence that followed Carlos' revelation was deafening. Both the Coach and Carlos looked at their respective coffee cups, neither willing to say a word as this deeply painful moment sunk in. Finally, it was the Coach who spoke. "Carlos, I don't know what to say other than thank you for sharing this story with me."

Carlos eventually regained his composure and explained the rest of the story. His father died in prison — after being arrested for drug smuggling. He never knew that he even had a son, and Carlos never knew his father.

Then he said, "I have another confession to tell you, Coach."

"OK."

"I always wanted a real father, like other kids at school. I wanted to play catch with my dad, hold his hand, and ask him questions."

"Sure."

"It wasn't until I played basketball for you for four years at school that I realized what that might be like. You were always there for all of us, especially me, and I... ." Carlos' voice fell off as he stared at the table.

"You what?"

The pause was lengthy, "I thought about what it might be like to be your son," Carlos said, and then stopped speaking..

The Coach cleared his throat, "Well, Carlos, I'm — I'm so surprised, touched — and honored, Carlos," he said, reaching his hand across the table to cover Carlos' hand. "I can't tell you how honored I am."

Chapter 13
Drill and Practice

Jim Talon walked into Carlos' office one morning early, before the rest of the team got in. "Carlos, this is the big one," he said sitting down with his coffee.

Startled, Carlos looked up, "Hey, Jim. What did you say?"

"We just won a big new piece of business."

"Great news!"

"Yep. Now you and your team have to deliver. No piece of cake on this one."

Jim sipped his coffee and then told Carlos the story about the business for whom they would be consulting. The aging owner of this business, Jeremiah Stanton, had stepped down about eighteen months ago and let his son, Jason, run the commercial real estate business at The Jeremiah Stanton Company. Not only had the real estate market gone south in a hurry, but Jason, a spoiled rich kid in his early thirties with an MBA from Harvard, thought far more about his CEO status than the business. He considered himself a creative, visionary genius, above such mundane issues as having to deal with customer satisfaction. The result: The company was bleeding profit from every open pore of its corporate body. Meanwhile, Jason continued to spend money on luxuries like outlandishly expensive Oriental rugs and designer leather chairs while the company's market share nosedived.. And to help Jason spend more money even faster than he made it, he brought in a buddy of his from prep school, also with an MBA, who possessed a similar attitude of entitlement.

It was the company's aging accountant who had blown the whistle on the plummeting financial situation to

Jeremiah, who now lived in Naples, Florida. Ironically, following his exit from the company, Jeremiah had turned a deaf ear to the business in order to transform himself from being a workaholic to a playaholic. He'd played golf, gone on trips, and walked the beach—all very vigorously. But all that changed when his accountant called and gave him the stark news. The following week, Jeremiah called Jim Talon, whom he'd worked with before when Talon helped the company get through a previous rough spot. Jim pulled together a quick proposal overnight—because of the critical nature of the situation—and e-mailed it to Jeremiah, who had accepted it immediately with no negotiation, to Jim's great surprise.

"I wrote an equal-skin-in-the-game contract for him."

"What?"

"I told him, if he paid half the fee up front, a healthy one at that, that he could pay us only what he thought it was worth when the job was finished."

"Huh?"

"Theoretically, for the second half of the consulting engagement, he could pay us nothing, full price, or any fraction thereof."

"Kind of a pay-to-play deal?"

"More like a pay-to-win deal!"

Jim explained that Jeremiah had already fired Jason's prep-school buddy but would not fire his son. However, he did put him in a kind of artificial receivership—in the corporate hands of JTS, Inc., and more specifically, in Carlos' and his team's hands. This meant that from this point forward, Jason Stanton could not spend a dollar without authorization from Carlos.

"Welcome to the acting chairman's job at The Jeremiah Stanton Company," Jim said as he stood to walk away.

"What? I mean wait a minute, Jim," Carlos said as he himself stood to get any parting words of wisdom from his boss.

"Can't wait. Gather up your team when they get in. I'll give you guys a quick briefing, and then you all are going to meet with Jason. Wish I could be there for that, but I have another piece of business I'm working on."

The rest of the team, except Mary who was working from home and phoned in, sat in the JTS conference room while Jim gave them the financial, administrative, and operational background of the company. He told them all the history from when Jeremiah had run the firm, through the economic downturn, and where it now sat financially. Roger dug into the financials, and Janice went for the operations and strategic plan, grilling Jim with questions — too many of which he could only shrug his shoulders. Half-looking at his watch he said, "Carlos, you and your team figure it out from here." And with that, he left for his next appointment.

Carlos wanted to run but was too stunned to move. This was a large contract, and the company needed to handle it successfully, but he would be pitting himself against a silver-spooned Ivy-Leaguer. In his mind it was a David-and-Goliath mismatch, and Carlos didn't even own a slingshot!

~

The next afternoon Carlos and the team, minus Mary, sat in the oak-paneled conference room of The Jeremiah Stanton Company, Jason on one side of the table, Carlos, Janice, and Roger on the other side. "OK, let's get this over quickly. My father wants oversight, and we're going to give him what he needs to see. And here's how it's going to work..."

"Whoa, Jason. Let's slow it down," Carlos said, trying to be as diplomatic as possible.

"I don't have time. I'm leaving for New York City in an hour for the weekend."

"Then I think we need to reschedule a meeting the minute you get back."

"I don't have time for that. Let's just paint by the numbers, shall we?"

"Paint by the numbers?"

"Look, we both know that you all are less qualified to advise me than first-year students at a second-tier business school. I simply won't waste my time."

Carlos looked at his team, who waited for what he might say. The silence extended for about twenty seconds, which seemed like an hour. Then Carlos pulled out his BlackBerry and said calmly, "Jason, I see that you have some strong feelings about this arrangement that your father set up."

"My father's an old man who's lost it…"

"Please, let me finish," Carlos said, holding up his hand like a traffic cop at a busy intersection. When Jason stopped, almost stunned, Carlos lowered his hand.

"To settle the way your father wants things to run, I'm just going to dial him up right now and put him on speaker phone, so you can express to him, as clearly as you just did to us, the way YOU believe this relationship should work." Without moving his eyes from Jason, he hit a speed dial button. It rang once, twice. And then Jason blinked and said, "OK. Turn it off."

With that, the meeting turned into much more of a give and take that lasted for two hours. When the team left the meeting and were driving back to the office, Roger said, "Wow, Carlos, that was a gutsy move, calling his father. I didn't know you knew old man Stanton."

"I don't."

"But you had his number on speed dial."

"Not really, I dialed my own apartment!"

Janice let out a roar, "No kidding! What would you have done if he didn't stop you?"

"Not sure. Just thought he'd fold."

"Really?" said Roger.

"I've played a lot of poker in college to make money for my tuition.. I knew he was bluffing."

"How?" asked Janice.

"He scratched his nose and shifted his position when he told me he was going to New York City."

"And?" said Janice.

"In poker, we call that a 'tell.' He was telling me something without actually saying it—that he was bluffing about going to New York."

"Wow!" Roger said.

"I made a lot of tuition money in my life off guys from top-tier schools," Carlos said, smiling.

～

When they returned to the office, they met in the conference room, with Mary on speakerphone, to figure out their game plan.

Janice spoke first. "Well, this'll be a real challenge."

"No doubt," said Roger.

Then, Carlos started to summarize the situation and asked others to chime in if he missed anything. The others nodded at the way Carlos seemed to grasp the severity and complexity of the situation, the arrogance of the son, and the intent of the father to get this business back on track—without the father's day-to-day intervention. In short, Jeremiah liked living in Florida and didn't want to come back to run the company — but needed the income to remain in the sunshine!

Then Carlos paused and asked, "So what do think we should do?"

Roger spoke first, "We need to analyze the data. Look at every account. Do an audit of the books. Start off with a baseline as a benchmark for progress."

"Great idea, Roger," Carlos said.

"I'd like to look over their strategic plan, if they have one, and see where they are on implementing it or not," said Janice.

"I'll try to synthesize whatever you and Roger find," Carlos said.

"And, I'll pull together a report of all the findings in a report that we can give to Mr. Stanton, his son, and Jim in a couple of weeks to let them know our plan for moving forward — after you guys give me whatever you find," Mary said.

"Sounds like a plan," said Carlos as he stood up to leave.

"A good one, I'd say," Janice said, smiling at Carlos.

"A damned good *team* effort," Carlos said, heading out the door.

Chapter 14
The Training Table

Hank was pouring Wally a cup of coffee when the Coach came in and sat down at the counter. "Well, finally, where have you been? It's been a few days," said Wally.

"Writing."

"You?" Hank said in raising his eyebrows.

"Yes, me. What's so strange about me writing?"

"Never really thought you wrote, other than play diagrams on a white board," Wally piped in.

"Just shows how little you guys know me. I used to write short stories and in college was a feature reporter for my college paper."

"So, what are you writing, Shakespeare?" Wally said as Hank filled the Coach's coffee cup and slid some cream and sugar toward the cup of steaming coffee.

"It's kinda personal," the Coach said, reaching for the cream.

"I see," Hank said.

"Ah, for God's sake, Coach. We're retired, not much going on and now when you got something juicy, you're gonna plead the Fifth Amendment on us!" Wally said, staring at the Coach. "Come on!"

The Coach drank some coffee and measured his words. "I've been thinking about Emma."

Hank looked at Wally with a look that said: *You dummy, now look what you started.*

The Coach caught the glance. "No, it's not a bad thing. I was just thinking about never having any kids." Then the Coach told them about his meetings with Carlos, especially this last meeting that they'd had — more specifically about the fact that Carlos had never had a father and how he'd always thought about the Coach as a bit of a surrogate father.

"So, I'm thinking about what I would have told my son, if I had one, about life and all that."

"Advice, you mean? Like never spit into the wind, never kiss a woman leaning away from you, or never, ever eat yellow snow!" Wally said, roaring with laughter at his own words.

"I guess those could be words to live by, but I was thinking about some of the things I learned coaching — and especially what I learned when Emma died."

"OK, like what?" Hank asked.

"You guys remember Mr. Ling?" the Coach asked.

"The guy who ran the dry cleaners next to the drug store?"

"Yeah. Turns out he was a war hero in Vietnam."

"Mr. Ling? Get out of town!" Wally said.

"Yep, he won the Navy Cross."

"The only thing higher is the Medal of Honor," said Hank.

"Mr. Ling taught me how to win state championships."

Wally pivoted in his seat toward the Coach. "That little guy — the drycleaner. He taught YOU how to coach basketball?"

"Yeah, well, indirectly."

"This I gotta hear this...spill it, Coach," Wally said, then motioned for Hank to pour him more coffee.

The Coach began with when Emma was in the final stages of her illness and not expected to live much longer. The Coach had been down in the dumps for months. One day he brought his dry cleaning to Mr. Ling, who had always been friendly and very respectful of the Coach.

This particular day, Mr. Ling was not at his shop, but his cousin had come to help out for a few days. The Coach asked where Mr. Ling was — recognizing that the man had not missed a day's work at the dry cleaning shop in decades.

The cousin explained that he was attending a ceremony at the White House — something about some decoration he was receiving for heroism in Vietnam. He saved some men but had never been put in for a medal of valor because his commander had been killed in the war and the records got lost. Years went by and everyone forgot, except one soldier whose life Mr. Ling had saved. When he was dying himself, this soldier wrote his senator about Ling and got the ball rolling.

The weeks following that conversation about Mr. Ling had been a blur for the Coach because Emma died. The Coach made all the arrangements, hosted the two families that came to town to mourn, and when it was all over and he'd returned to an empty house, the Coach promptly fell apart.

About a week later, the Coach was picking up his laundry at the dry cleaners. Mr. Ling stood behind the counter as usual, the Coach explained to Wally and Hank. "Stood there, just like he had for the past twenty years."

Mr. Ling expressed his condolences, and the Coach thanked him. Then the Coach talked about Mr. Ling's medal, which embarrassed Ling. So he quickly changed the subject back to himself and basketball.

"That was the first time I ever told anyone I was thinking about quitting the team."

"What?" Wally said, stunned by this revelation. He looked at Hank, who shrugged. "We knew you had decided to take the year off when Emma died, but quitting the team? That's news."

"I was pretty depressed back then. Worst time of my life."

The Coach continued his story.

He explained how Mr. Ling started to offer the Coach tea every time he came in, which became a kind of weekly ritual. As they got to know each other better, the Coach asked Mr. Ling about his tour in Vietnam. At first Ling would not talk much about what he'd done in the war. But as they got to know each other better, both opened up.

Ling told the Coach that he'd always been a shy and small boy. His father had taught him the martial arts so he could defend himself against bigger boys, especially bullies at school. And after college, Ling decided to join the Marine Corps. He talked about the Marine Corps Officers Candidate School and the Basic School at Quantico. From the very beginning, the drill sergeants picked on Ling because he was small—the runt of the litter. They kept telling him to give up now—all part of the hazing program. But at the time, Ling didn't understand how the game was played and took it very personally. He also had trouble making his uniform fit properly, largely because he was so small.. This weakness, like any weaknesses in any of the other recruits, did not get overlooked by the experienced drill sergeants who called him "a soup sandwich," the "tiny man," "Little Ling," and a host of other names.

But on the first day of their three-mile run, Ling took off like he was shot out of a cannon. Only one other guy even stayed within a quarter mile of him, an all-American in college, who had run track as an undergraduate. Next came the combat obstacle course, the torturous Hill Trail, and then one physical obstacle after another. The drill sergeants were amazed but embarrassed by their initial assessment and underestimation of Ling. So, they minimized Ling's accomplishments and focused on his shortcomings, like marksmanship, military bearing, and land navigation — Ling was awful when it came to finding his way around with a map and a compass.

But through all the hazing, Ling kept his cool. Always very respectful, he took the abuse but kept his mind on the prize — finishing OCS and getting his commission. One day on the training field, everyone was in a circle doing physical training with pugil sticks, a five-foot pole with heavy, padded weights on either end. Each contestant wore a protective helmet and, when called, stepped into the middle of the large circle of officer candidates to do battle. The first five pairs of opponents got jeers and hoots, as one after the other won and lost. Finally, a big guy named "Stash" Drembroski stepped into the circle and annihilated the next three opponents.

That was when the drill sergeant tapped Ling on the shoulder and told him to go in against the big Polish kid from Chicago. Ling nodded deferentially and did as he was told. Everyone prepared to watch a massacre, especially the two drill sergeants who were snickering to each other. Drembroski charged like a Brahma bull at the much smaller Ling who stood his ground until the exact last moment, when he sidestepped the big hulk who crashed into the ground to the utter surprise of everyone watching. An angry, embarrassed Polish bull, Drembroski dusted himself off and charged again, this time with a bit more tactical approach. But as he engaged Ling, the big guy was hit four times so fast that it knocked his breath out, and he found himself on the ground. Ling tried to help him up, but the big guy was too embarrassed to accept aid.

When he finally got up, Drembroski came at Ling again only to be pummeled so fast that it was almost difficult to see what Ling was doing. The sergeants were shocked but not as shocked as Drembroski, who lay in a heap, nearly unconscious. After that, Ling received no further harassment from the drill sergeants.. He finished at the top of his class both at OCS and then at The Basic School located at Camp Barrett on the Quantico Marine Base.

His first command as a lieutenant in Vietnam was a repeat of the same thing. Everyone snickered when they first saw him. Ling told the Coach that being underestimated had always been his greatest advantage. His father had taught him that Westerners had always been louder and bolder — they came in like heroes always trying to save the day, like John Wayne. That's why they were always stunned by quiet "sleepers" like Mr. Ling.

The Coach explained to Wally and Hank how Mr. Ling taught him about a great Chinese philosopher, Lau Tzu, and the great book he wrote, the *Tao Te Ching*.

"The what?" Wally asked, leaning on the counter of the coffee shop.

"I'll tell you about it next time we meet. I gotta get going," the Coach said, finishing the last sip of his coffee.

"Sure, get us all primed up, and then leave," Wally said.

"Talk to you soon," the Coach said, leaving an extra dollar on the counter for Hank.

Chapter 15
The Rematch

When Jason Stanton entered the conference room to meet with Carlos for a one-on-one meeting, he slapped down his notebook on the table harder than he needed to. "Good morning," Carlos said.

"Maybe for you and your goons."

"What?"

"This Roger, who works for you. He's asked for ALL our books."

"That's what he's supposed to do—conduct a baseline audit of all the accounts. It's a place for us to start. Standard stuff."

The argument was on. Steamed at being audited, Jason took a number of verbal punches at Carlos, his team, and JTS itself. Carlos listened quietly, deferentially, but through it all remained poker faced. When Jason had finished, he looked at Carlos and asked, "Well?"

Carlos simply said, "I'm sorry you feel that way."

"That's it, you're sorry!"

"And that I honor what your family has done for the business all these years."

"Honor? What the hell are you talking about?"

Carlos measured his words and began to explain. "Your dad built his company from the ground up. And he believed that you were ready to take it to the next level."

"Yeah, and that went into the crapper pretty quick."

Carlos laughed briefly and continued, "He just wants you, himself, and the employees to continue to prosper."

"OK, what's that got to do with honor?"

"To quote an old coach of mine: 'Humility and honor help us all to respect another's talents while also recognizing our own strengths and challenges.'"

"What if I don't feel humble?" he said.

"Nobody can make you feel humility. But, without it, honor won't work."

"Big deal."

"It is a big deal."

For the next five minutes, the two of them bandied back and forth about honor.

"Look, Carlos, you don't make me feel humble. The opposite, in fact."

"Good. That's at least a place to start."

"Whatever!" Jason said and got up to leave.

~

A file tucked under his right arm, Roger came into Carlos' office a couple of weeks after his audit had started. He looked tired. He explained that Jason had been fighting him every inch of the way. When Roger asked for account information, he normally got the runaround. Jason, he knew, was not giving him all the information he needed, and frankly the money just wasn't adding up. Roger was stymied.

Carlos asked him if he'd talked to the accountant who had originally turned in the complaint to Jeremiah, the founder. Roger had talked to the retired accountant but felt that he had been holding back—like he knew something he didn't want to admit.

"Do you have his phone number?" Carlos asked.

Roger looked into the file he was holding and wrote down a number on a piece of paper. Carlos called the number several times that day but did not want to leave a message. On his final attempt late in the day, Roy Alston answered. Carlos explained that he needed to meet with him, just a formality, and asked if they could meet for coffee later that night, around 9:00 P.M., at a shop not far from Alston's neighborhood. Alston agreed.

Carlos got to the coffee shop about fifteen minutes before Alston and sat so that he could see the front door. Then he waited. At 9:03 a short, balding man in his sixties entered. Carlos sensed immediately that it was Alston, so he got up and waved to the accountant. The two introduced themselves and sat down after Alston got some coffee.

When Alston was settled, Carlos began to dig into the issue. "Mr. Alston, thanks so much for alerting us to the excessive spending at the company."

"Please call me Roy. I just couldn't watch the company that Jeremiah had built over forty years get whittled down to nothing by those kids."

"Jason and his prep-school friend, I assume?"

"Yes," he said shaking his head.

"What were some of the things Jason did that pointed to that?"

"He spent money like a drunken sailor. Bought everything he wanted…always the best of the best. Couldn't just have a BMW but had to have a 700 series—for a company car!"

"We've managed to track many of those kinds of purchases, thanks to you."

Alston took a swallow of his coffee and then nodded affirmatively.

"But, Roy, we're still coming up short in cash reserves—about a half a million, my best analyst says."

"Really?" Alston said, shifting in his seat and drawing his right hand to his mouth.

"Does that surprise you?"

"Not the way this kid spends money. No."

"Could there be an account somewhere that we're not finding? A place he may have hidden the money?"

Roy shifted in his chair again and then cleared his throat. "I have no idea in what sub-account the slick MBA from Harvard might have hidden the money."

"Sub-account?"

Roy stared at Carlos, "I don't know where he stuck the money or where he took it from. I'm just guessing he tried to hide it in a sub-account."

"I see."

"Do you have any best guesses where we might find the money?"

"No, not really. I have no idea where Mr. Cool would hide it."

The two talked for a while longer, but when Carlos realized that Roy Alston had run dry on leads for the team, he thanked Roy and asked if he could contact him again if he had any more questions.

"Yes, of course," he said. "In fact, let me know how it's going from time to time."

"I will."

~

The next day, when Roger came into work, he looked beat.

"You look like you've had a tough day," Carlos said.

"Playing the find-a-needle-in-the-haystack game trying to find that money."

"I thought all analysts loved that game."

"Yeah, for the first forty hours or so, then it gets old."

They talked for a bit about the series of findings. Roger, though frustrated he could not find the half-million, had concluded that the downturn in the company's finances were due mostly to the combination of the tough economic times and Jason's unfettered spending habits.

"I'm not so sure," said Carlos.

"What?"

"First, a half-million isn't like loose change."

"Yeah, but the way this kid spent. Fast, sloppy, and no receipts."

"True. But my interview with the accountant was a little strange."

"Oh, yeah, you saw him last night. What happened?"

"I can't quite say but some of his responses were, well, odd."

"How so?"

Carlos described how eager Roy was in the beginning of the interview to point the finger directly at Jason, and likely for good reason.

"But when I asked him about the half-million, he hemmed and hawed — his whole demeanor changed. Suddenly he became very dumb. Didn't know this or that. Probably that damned Jason again…sort of routine."

Carlos explained that growing up on the streets, you learned how to read people quickly or you could get hurt. And how playing poker in college — with his street smarts — he had paid many a tuition bill. Yes, there was something strange with the way Roy answered the questions. And the 'sub-account' reference had struck Carlos as more than casual.

Chapter 16
Chalk Talk

Tony's restaurant was more crowded than usual, and the Coach was already seated and sipping his water when Carlos entered. The Coach stood and gave him a shake and a shoulder bump—the classic man-hug. But this time the Coach held the hug longer than he had in the past. The waitress swooped right in and got their orders—which by now she knew by heart.

As they ate, Carlos explained the old accountant's odd comments, and the way he responded to Carlos' questions.

"You have great instincts, Carlos. You always did as a point guard too. Just one caution—don't assume the conclusion."

"What?"

"There could be any number of things that made him respond the way he did. Just don't assume either the best or the worst, and you'll be better off."

"Good point, I guess."

"You guess? OK, let's play a game."

"A game?"

"Just a quick one."

"OK."

"Look at that table in the corner. See the man leaning into the table and talking to that woman?"

"Yes."

"Good. Now watch the conversation."

Carlos did. It looked romantic, then it got heated. The guy stiffened up and started to point his finger. The woman countered with an equally stern face. Suddenly, no more conversation as they drank their coffee.

"Tell me what you see."

Carlos leaned back from his observer's position and said, "They had a fight."

"I'm guessing you're right. Anything else?"

"Not that I could see."

"So, if you had to testify in court, what could you say?"

"Not much, just how they looked. Their gestures. That sort of stuff."

"Correct. First you need to know more stuff. Maybe how they were related. What their history was. What the conversation was about. You'd have to learn more about what was going on. And how could you do that?"

"I could ask the waiter?" Carlos added, shrugging his shoulders.

"Great idea! Find out if they're regulars. Maybe they're well known to the entire staff, including the hostess."

"Another lead…talk to her?"

"How about yourself?"

"What about me?" Carlos asked.

"What's your experience with arguing with someone?"

"Well, never thought about that. But when my mother used to argue with her sister, I felt pretty uncomfortable."

"Do you see that how you view arguing might make you more or less sensitive to the situation you were watching?"

"I guess."

"You ARE the information filter. If you hate arguing, you're likely more sensitive to it than most people. That could mean you have a great detector—or that you're seeing arguing when it's not always there."

"Interesting. Not sure how I feel about it. But definitely interesting."

The Coach said that in good coaching you had to know a lot about yourself, the other coach, the sport itself, how to learn more, and how to teach it to your team.

"I call it the five Ks," the Coach said.

Carlos pulled out his small blue notebook. Paging to the marker, Carlos said, "So, we have five C's of Good Character: Candor, Communication, Commitment, Consistency, and Courage — correct?"

"That's right. I'm impressed you've written it down."

Then Carlos turned the page to show the Coach the five H's: Honor Self, Others, Company, Community, and Country.

"Again, I'm impressed, son," the Coach said, almost blushing as he realized what he'd called Carlos. Then the Coach cleared his throat. "So today I've got five things you have to know to have Good Sense — to add to your notebook," he said.

"Cool, five K's of Good Sense — so, shoot. What are they?"

The Coach recited the five K's while Carlos wrote them down in his black playbook:

Good Sense

1. Know yourself

2. Know others

3. Know your stuff

4. Know how to learn

5. Know how to teach

"The first K is to know yourself. Self-awareness is one of the really tough ones," the Coach said, as he shifted his position slightly to look at Carlos more directly.

"Of all the players I ever coached, I think you were the most self-aware."

"Thanks, Coach, I think."

The Coach told Carlos how some of the great players he'd coached had actually hurt the team. Some had over-inflated opinions of how well they played and their arrogance made others on the team jealous, even angry. And other great players had the opposite problem. "You remember Ricky Albright? He was a very talented kid but he never had the confidence to take the shot, even when he was wide open."

"Yeah, sure, I remember Ricky—always passed the ball."

"You were different. You knew what you could do and what you couldn't. You knew when to shoot the three-pointer and when to pass it off."

"I guess."

"I *know*, Carlos. But, sometimes you didn't get to know others on the floor—especially the guys you didn't like."

"What do you mean?"

"Just take a minute and think about who on the team drove you the most crazy."

"Brendan Fletcher!"

"Yep. Sure he was a big showboat...cocky."

"It's been years since I thought of that jerk!"

"Exactly! When you didn't like someone you shut down, gave up on Brendan—only passed to him when you HAD to."

"He was a big hot dog."

"Yes, I know, but Brendan knew a lot of stuff about basketball. You could have learned a lot from him."

Carlos thought a bit as he took a sip of his water. Then he looked at the Coach and said, "I did shut him out—in spite of what you told me at the time."

"And what was the result?" the Coach asked, holding up his hand like a stop sign, "You don't have to answer right now."

Then the Coach described a half-dozen players on his teams, who had gone through problems in their personal lives during high school, including Brendan, whose father had left the family when Brendan was only eight years old.

"I had no idea," said Carlos.

"So, maybe if you had known that, Brendan might have made more sense to you?"

"No doubt. But why didn't you tell me?"

"I couldn't. Brendan made me swear I wouldn't tell anyone."

Then, the Coach noted that knowing who you are and knowing about others on your team and being empathetic—whether it was a basketball team or a work team—were the very foundation of Good Sense.

"So, know yourself, know others, and what...know your stuff? I could have learned even more if I tried to understand Brendan better?"

"Yes. You had a lot of talent but lacked some of the fundamental knowledge of the game—because you took it up so late in life. Soccer really was your game."

"Football, we call it in my country."

"See, I need to know more stuff to be more credible," the Coach said, smiling at Carlos. "Leaders have to know the sport or type of work that their teams are engaged in. Take your job. If you'd never done management consulting, leading your group would be very difficult."

"So, do I have to be the best consultant to be the leader?"

"No. In fact, superstars often don't make the best leaders or coaches, and the reverse is true. Look at historically great pro football coaches like Joe Gibbs of the Washington Redskins. You just have to know your stuff — you don't have to have been the superstar on the field."

Then the Coach explained the last two K's together. Leaders have to be able and willing to learn new things — to keep their knowledge base up to snuff. They have to read, develop mentors, take courses, and volunteer to stretch themselves by taking on difficult assignments. And then they have to be willing and able to share what they've learned with people who work for them. Good leaders have to become not only good learners but also good mentors and teachers.

"Acquiring and spreading knowledge to the team are fundamental to a leader and a team's success," the Coach said. "If the coach, I mean leader, doesn't keep his team current, the world will pass him or her by, eventually make the team irrelevant."

Carlos wrote quickly in his coaching notebook as the Coach spoke. And when he looked up, the Coach was grinning.

"What?"

"No, nothing, I'm sorry."

"Really, what are you thinking?"

The coach hesitated and then spoke, "Well, here we are talking about learning and teaching — and that's exactly what's going on — here, NOW." Carlos looked down at his notebook, then at his pen, then at the Coach.

"Yep…so it is," he said as he wrote down the five K's: Know Self, Others, Your Stuff, How to Learn, How to Teach.

After he finished writing, Carlos started to close the notebook, but the Coach reached across the table and put his hand in the way. "Hold on, there's something more that needs to be said."

Carlos looked up as the Coach explained that to have complete trust in anyone, that person had to have not just one or even two legs of The Trust Triangle but all three of them. With that the coach drew out a sketch of the triangle in Carlos' notebook.

"I'm not exactly sure what you're saying, Coach," said Carlos, "Do you mean that it's all or nothing?"

"Yes. Now there's no one single person who scores high in every aspect of the Trust Triangle, but if you're not at least solid in all three…good character, good sense, and good will, getting people to really trust you is not possible."

The Coach told Carlos how he'd worked with teachers who were smart (had good sense), who even had good character, but who were jealous of the basketball program when he coached at the school. So, the Coach never quite trusted them to back the program.

"Yeah," said Carlos, "like when I first went to work at the consulting firm. I had a mentor who retired soon after I got there. He was a nice guy, smart, but his head was out the door looking at retirement, and I never felt he cared about my future. I never did really trust him."

"I think you get the idea, Carlos."

"Yes, I do, and thanks, Coach, for always being there for me!"

With that, Carlos completed the notes in his blue notebook:

Good Sense (The Five K's)

In his/her daily actions, a leader demonstrates that she/he:

1. Knows self—own strengths and challenges

2. Knows others' individual strengths and challenges and has empathy

3. Knows stuff—the core elements of his/her job or profession

4. Knows how to learn/acquire new knowledge and skills

5. Knows how to and wants to teach new knowledge and skills to others

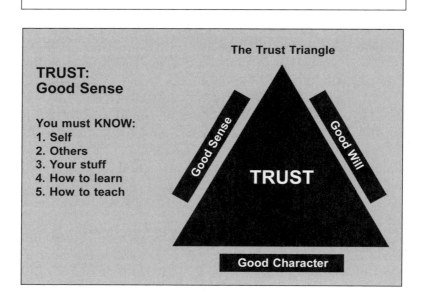

The Trust Triangle

TRUST: Good Sense

You must KNOW:
1. Self
2. Others
3. Your stuff
4. How to learn
5. How to teach

Good Sense

Good Will

TRUST

Good Character

Chapter 17
A New Coaching Plan

When the Coach sat down at the counter, Hank was taking an order and did not see him. The Coach pulled his notebook out of his pocket and made some notes in it.

Shortly after, Wally entered with his usual fanfare. When he'd sat down, Hank turned around.

"Coach, didn't see you sitting there until the human megaphone came in!"

The Coach just nodded and took the menu in hand as Wally held forth. "More on these damned buyouts. I'm thinking about starting a business, tanking it, and then asking the feds to bail me out."

The Coach just listened.

"Remember that old Peter Sellers movie, *The Mouse that Roared,* about the country that was going bankrupt? They declared war on the U.S., knowing that we'd bail them out after we won the war!"

"Sounds like a plan, Einstein. What are you having today?"

"Usual."

After the men got settled into their meals and Hank made his way back to the corner of the counter—the clubhouse section of the diner—the men started to chatter about a wide range of subjects, from the Redskins to the Caps and from finance to welfare. Finally, Wally piped up, "Say Coach, you were going to 'splain that Chinese book— The Toe-de-something-or-other."

The Coach laughed and then said, the *Tao Te Ching*.

"Whatever. How about just telling us what the hell it's all about."

The Coach winced and then began to explain. "First," he said, "it's the *Tao Te Ching*...the book about life."

"Nothing like a nice narrow topic...LIFE," Wally said, grabbing another cup of coffee. "This is going to take a while!"

The Coach ignored him and told the history of the book. Written by Lao Tzu, an ancient Chinese philosopher, in 500 B.C., the Tao was basically intended as an instruction manual to the leaders of a divided China during the warring states period of its history. In only eighty-one verses, Lao Tzu teaches with humble, pristine clarity a new model of leadership quite different from western leadership. So powerful is the *Tao Te Ching* that it has been translated into nearly as many languages as the Bible. Consisting of only 5,000 Chinese characters, many of which are not even used today, the Tao has been interpreted by many scholars.

"OK, so what does it teach? What did you learn that changed your coaching? I mean for God's sake. You won five state championships in a row."

"Mr. Ling helped me understand the Tao," the Coach replied. "Give me a minute," and with that, he began to write a list in his notebook:

- The Tao itself is the indefinable energy force in the universe.

- People (especially leaders) need to be

    - Selfless—Suppress their egos.
    - Humble and not the center of attention.
    - Centered on the internal world, not reactive to the external world.
    - Yielding to the will of others, not domineering.
    - Contemplative, not assertive. Allowing others to be all they can be.

- Inclusive and never exclusive.
- Silent and ever listening before commenting.
- Less, not more—avoiding excess in all things.
- Soft like water, not hard like rock.
- Servant leader rather than hero leader.
- Both Yin and Yang—feminine and masculine.

When he'd finished his list, the Coach slid it over to Wally and said, "Here you go."

Wally looked it over. "Looks like a lot of psycho mumbo jumbo. Can you give me the bottom line, Coach?"

"Sure," Hank answered. "In short, the Tao is NOT like you, Wally!"

It took a second for Wally to get the barb, but Hank had already lost it and was laughing so hard he could hardly catch his breath, saying, "I think I could use some oxygen!"

When all the laughing stopped, the Coach got more serious. "When Emma died, I took a good look inside myself. You remember, I took a year off from coaching. That was the year I met Mr. Ling, and when he taught me about the Tao." The Coach took a sip of water as Wally and Hank just looked on. No barbs were flying now.

"I realized that I had been kind of a hero-coach," he continued. "Always trying to lead from the front—with a shining shield with a big H on it for Hero! Always charging forward. But after I learned to step back and allow others to take center stage, I started trusting the team to do the right thing. That's when the game changed for me. I didn't coach basketball…I WAS basketball."

Wally couldn't help himself. "Coach, careful now, you're sounding a little nutty."

"I know it. Not controlling my world but *being* in the world taught me more than I could have ever hoped for. It helped me get past Emma's death, past my own self-pity, and past owning the team."

"Owning?" asked Hank.

"Yeah, most coaches, especially folks who've been coaching for a long time, start thinking that they own the team. That's why they take the losses so personally — their lifetime records, all that sort of stuff."

"Yeah, but how else can you rate a coach except win-loss?"

"I started by thinking like the Tao. What was the essence of a team? The players. To me the kids became the focus. What was most important for them became my mantra."

"So, how'd that get you to win?"

"I hired Mr. Ling as my assistant coach."

"I never saw him on the bench."

"He refused to…he's a shy guy. He actually never came to a practice. When I came to get my laundry every week, we talked, and I asked his advice."

"And?" asked Hank.

"He wrote out the seventeenth verse of the Tao for me."

And with that the Coach pulled out a laminated card with Chinese on one side and English printing on the other:

The *Tao Te Ching*: 17th Verse

With the greatest leader above them,
People barely know one exists.
Next comes one whom they love and praise.
Next comes one whom they fear.
Next comes one whom they despise and defy.

When a leader trusts no one,
No one trusts him.

The great leader speaks little.
He never speaks carelessly.
He works without self-interest and leaves no trace.
When all is finished, the people say,
"We did it ourselves."

Both Hank and Wally read the script on the laminated card and then looked back to the Coach.

"Mr. Ling kept me focused on the kids. I got involved in their lives, on and off the court. They became like sons to me. And that made all the difference."

Chapter 18
Going on the Offensive

Before Carlos met with Jason again, he wanted to know much more about him and take advantage of the advice the Coach had offered at their last Wednesday meeting: Know others. It wasn't that difficult to find out a lot about Jason because he had been active at the business school—in fact had served as treasurer of his class at business school. Interesting, thought Carlos. In all the research Carlos got on Jason, there was never a word of impropriety about his time as treasurer. Jason seemed to do a good job at the position, by all accounts in the student newspaper and fraternity newsletters archived on the Internet.

After an hour or more, Carlos found a list of Jason's fraternity brothers. The list included current business contact numbers, so he decided to call a few, posing as a headhunter vetting a client—which in a sense he was. He was only able to get two people who commented briefly but both of whom called Jason scrupulous when it came to minding the financial shop of the fraternity. After collecting as much information as he could without raising too many red flags, Carlos scheduled a meeting with Jason the following day.

They met in the company conference room. Jason entered a few minutes late, greeted Carlos stiffly, and sat down. "OK, let's get this over with, shall we," Jason sniped.

"I'll try to keep this as brief as possible, but I have some questions for you to answer, and I'm bound by the audit to have them answered. So, we'll need as much time as it takes. Can we be clear on that expectation?"

Jason shifted and said, "Fine, let's just get started."

Carlos asked a number of fact-based questions: Who was appointed treasurer of the company? Who had access to the books? Jason answered them in a matter-of-fact way—expending only as much energy as possible. Then, Carlos got to the meat of the encounter.

"Jason, Roger found a deficit in your books of around a half-million dollars."

"What the hell! How much?"

"Half-million."

"Impossible!"

"Wish that were true, but it's not."

"We need to verify this—now!"

"There'll be time for all that. First, I want to ask you if you know Roy Alston."

"That crazy old crank. He's been sucking away salary from my father for over forty years."

"Well, he claims that you were spending the company into the toilet."

"He's a myopic old man. No vision. Head stuck in a ledger account. Useless."

"Frankly, he had a similarly negative opinion about your handling of the company."

"What exactly did he say?"

"That you and your cohort from prep school spent money loose and free."

"I'll admit that I'm no miser. I confess that I like things to be first class, despite my father's, let's say, thriftiness."

Carlos moved his chair closer and leaned right into Jason's space and said, "Look, Mr. Alston told us about some secret sub-account that you might have set up."

"Secret sub-account! This sounds more bizarre by the minute."

"So, is it safe to say that you do not know of such a sub-account?"

"Damned right!" he said, pounding his fist on the table and staring deep into Carlos' eyes.

After more than a few seconds, Carlos blinked first and broke the silence. "OK, so for the record, you're saying that you knew nothing of such a sub-account."

"Yes, that's exactly what I'm saying."

"And, you would not mind if we brought in a forensics team to trace the money?"

"I'd welcome that...the sooner the better."

"How about taking a polygraph so we can clear up this issue?"

"It's insulting, but sure. The quicker I get this behind me, the better. On one condition, however."

"What's that?"

"You offer Roy Alston the same polygraph 'opportunity,'" Jason said gesturing the word "opportunity" with air quotes.

"Fair enough."

Jason nodded with a kind of smug satisfaction.

Carlos, a bit confused, said, "OK, thanks. I think that does it for now. Thanks for your time."

"Right," Jason said, thrusting back his chair from the table and then striding out of the conference room.

~

Later that day, Carlos met with Roger. When Carlos described his meeting with Jason, Roger said, "He's such an arrogant jerk."

"I won't argue that point, but I don't think he's a thief."

"I hear you. I'm shocked that he'd agree to take a polygraph."

"Yeah, that got to me, too. And the way he welcomed the auditor. Plus, he acted like an innocent guy. He was angry but cooperative."

"Now what?"

"I say we meet with Roy Alston."

~

The next afternoon, Roy Alston sat in the JTS conference room. He was alert, even smiling, when Carlos and Roger came in. After a friendly greeting, all three sat down. Roger sat off to the side taking notes, and Carlos sat directly across from Roy Alston.

"Mr. Alston..." Carlos started to say.

"Please, Carlos, call me Roy."

"Thank you. OK, Roy, first off, thanks for coming down here today and for all the help you have provided thus far."

"Of course.. Did you talk to Jason yet?"

"Yes."

"What'd he say? Did he fess up?"

"Not exactly."

"He's a jerk."

Roger shot a look at Carlos that said *See, I told you he was a jerk.*

"I'll admit that he can be a bit difficult."

"Well, what DID he say?"

"That he knew nothing about the money."

Then Carlos explained that Jason seemed confident and seemed to be telling the truth. He told Alston about Jason's willingness to bring in a forensic accountant and to take a polygraph.

"A forensic accountant? A polygraph?" Alston said, his tongue seeming to search inside his cheek for some moisture.

"Yes. We have a number of former FBI agents we hire in such matters."

"Really?"

"Yes. And as merely a formality to help round out this investigation, we'd like you also to take an elimination polygraph."

"Me. An elimination polygraph? What's that?"

Carlos explained that when serious allegations are made, that the person alleging the issue is routinely polygraphed to determine his or her veracity — to make sure no time is wasted chasing shadows. It's standard, a formality, Carlos explained, and it takes about an hour, sometimes two.

Alston shifted in his seat, picked a piece of lint from his jacket, wet his lips, but said nothing.

Carlos closed in on him, "Roy, is there something I need to know?"

Roy physically sat back in his chair, "No. I don't... think so."

"You don't think so? Then, maybe there is something?"

"Well...."

Carlos moved in so close that Roy started to sweat — just slightly over his right eyebrow.. "Roy, tell me what you know. Save us all a lot of time and having to call those FBI polygraph guys in."

"Look, I didn't mean any harm."

When Carlos sensed that Roy had broken, he pushed his chair away from him to let the pressure off just a bit. It was a safety valve technique he'd learned from an old forensic accounting guy he'd known.

"Jason's such a jackass."

"You'll get no fight from me on that description," Carlos said with a faint smile.

"It's just that he was dismantling everything his father and I had built. He was spending money recklessly, and I couldn't stand by and watch it. Jeremiah was in Florida playing shuffleboard, for God's sake."

Carlos just nodded.

Roy paused to take a sip of water from the glass that Carlos had pushed his way earlier. "He was pissing away everyone's retirement, including mine."

A long silence followed as Roy collected his thoughts and carefully chose his words.

"I just could NOT let him steal the money from all those loyal employees...I couldn't," he said as he dropped his head into his hands.

Carlos kept quiet and leaned in to touch Roy's shoulder.

Finally, when Roy had regained his composure, he spoke very methodically, "I could not let that little jerk steal the money, so I hid it safely in a sub-account, where he could not find it."

"Which sub-account?" asked Carlos.

"A sub-account attached to employee benefits. Takes a bit of hunting to find it, but I'll show you," Roy said in a voice that started to crack.

"Thank you, Roy. I really appreciate your fully explaining the situation. I certainly understand why you did it."

"Thank you, Carlos," Roy said as his voice cracked, and he sobbed into his hands.

Chapter 19
At the Buzzer

Tony's was crowded when the Coach arrived, and Carlos was seated at their table.

"Hey, Carlos, good to see you. How's it going?

With that, Carlos recounted his interviews with Jason and then with Roy. He took his time to review the interview details for the coach. And when he finished, the Coach lifted his water glass and toasted Carlos, "Excellent detective work, Carlos."

"Actually, it was the leadership coaching you gave me as much as anything."

"How so?"

Carlos explained that by showing his team (Janice, Roger and Mary) his Good Character through the five C's, he got their attention. After a rocky start, he'd been completely honest, communicated with them regularly to keep everyone informed, showed he was both committed and consistent in how he handled issues that came up, and finally showed courage confronting both Jason and Roy Alston to get to the truth.

"Nice work, I'd say."

"There's more. I followed your five K's of Good Sense as well. And by being completely honest with the team and asking them to do the same with me, I got feedback…did I ever! And you really helped me a lot as well. I have learned a lot about myself."

The coach nodded modestly.

"Then I got to know my team better by spending much more time with them, both as a group and individually. I've come to respect Roger's analytical skills, just as I think he sees my strategic planning skill. Together, we have vision and execution covered.".

Carlos stopped to take a sip and then said, "And Janice, well, she was a slower boil for me. But I came to appreciate her interest in information—sometimes even gossip. But I kept her on a short leash. And when I thought it was getting a bit much, we talked—communicated. I also began to focus on her keen strategic sense—which actually sharpened my ability in that area. And getting Roger and Janice on the same page with me helped all three of us understand and support Mary's home situation. In the end, we've become a close-knit group, and we're very profitable for the company."

"Great, Carlos. When you take the time to get to know other people, they take the time to get to know you. Reciprocity is universal."

"No doubt, Coach."

Then Carlos described how he was getting to "know his stuff" in the consulting field better by sticking close to Jim Talon, using him as his consulting coach. Carlos had also enrolled in several business-school online courses and had set up a pretty rigorous reading program for himself. And what was even better, he had not only learned "how to learn" but also was truly enjoying the process.

"Finally, I've been not only teaching some of the folks on the team, but Jim has also had me teaching some of the interns at the company. I've actually designed and been teaching a mentoring program. I can't tell you how great that's been. In fact, the more I teach, the more I learn."

The coach held up his beer glass and toasted Carlos. "Cheers, Carlos, you broke the code."

"The code?"

"About knowledge—Good Sense. The more you teach, the more you learn."

Then Carlos got a bit more serious. "You also taught me about Good Will, and I took that to heart. The word 'honor' has become an important word in my vocabulary. And the five H's were the key to breaking this case. I honored myself, and would take no less than the truth, however hard that would be for me or the company. I honored Roy and Jason—even when I would have rather shown Jason the door."

The coach laughed so hard that he nearly spit out his water.

"Sorry, Coach! But it's true. I also honored the company that Jeremiah started and especially my own company, JTS, and its responsibility to the community, the country, even this world in which we've all been given such great opportunities. You know, in the beginning, I thought this aspect of good will and honor to the community, country, and world—well, it sounded pretty lofty, but it's given me a broader scope to see where I and the company fit into the greater picture."

"Boy, it certainly sounds like you've thought this one through, Carlos."

"Yep. Sure have, Coach, thanks to you."

The coach nodded slightly to recognize the compliment.

"There are a couple of more things I want to tell you— and a couple of important questions to ask you."

The coach instinctively leaned forward.

"First off, Jim Talon just told me confidentially that he will retire in two more years."

"No kidding."

"And, he's hinted that he might consider me for managing partner—on the condition that he thinks I'm ready at the time."

"What a great vote of confidence, Carlos!" the Coach said, reaching across the table to shake his protégé's hand.

"Thanks, but it's going to be a tough job. Which leads me to my first question." Carlos paused and then looked directly into the Coach's eyes. "I want you to be my coach."

Confused, the Coach asked, "What do you mean?"

"I want you to coach me...be my personal executive coach."

"I'm no executive coach."

"Oh yes you are. Without your help, I'd have been lost. So how about it?"

The Coach hesitated for a long while as he looked at the silverware on the table.. Finally he said, "I think you're nuts, but I'm willing to talk to you like we've been doing."

"That's what I'm looking at...every other Wednesday night."

"Deal."

"I want to pay you."

"No deal!"

"But, Coach, you're providing me a service, and I want to pay you for it."

"Nope. But one thing you can pay for."

"Sure. What's that?"

"Dinner tonight. I forgot my wallet!"

"Deal," Carlos said laughing. "Now, for the last order of business. As you know, due to the economic downturn, a lot of federal, state, and local budgets have been slashed. I got a call from the principal at Weston Middle School to see if I or any of the former players from Arlington High would be interested in coaching the team. I told him that I would take the job, only if you work with me and the team."

The Coach froze in place and just stared at Carlos. At first Carlos looked at him and then turned away, thinking that he might have insulted the Coach. Finally, with a big grin the Coach said, "Carlos, I'd be honored to help you."

Carlos reached across the table and took the Coach's hand into both of his and said, "Great, Coach."

Chapter 20
Epilogue

The next two years sprinted by. Jim Talon retired as planned and promoted Carlos to president and CEO but Jim remained active as the chairman of the Board. Carlos promoted Roger to his old position, and Mary became one of his star performers — especially after she got her mother situated in a wonderful assisted-living facility. Janice formed her own strategic planning company — with JTS as her anchor client — again, thanks to Carlos.

Jason Stanton had finally gotten his father's permission to sell the company after getting the financials in order. After the sale, Jason took a job with a major consulting company in New York City. Jeremiah, Jason's father, enjoyed himself in Florida — and had convinced Roy Alston to join him there part time as a "snow bird" in the winters — while still keeping an active hand in the company.

Wally and Hank still got coffee with the Coach a few times a week — a bit less than before because of the Coach's new responsibilities. Carlos had engaged the Coach more and more into the company's fabric. He'd even been speaking to clients about coaching, of all things. And he'd been such a great success that clients had started asking for the Coach to speak at their corporate meetings. He'd become a bit of an unlikely and unwilling business celebrity.

The Coach had also been busy as an assistant coach to Carlos, who had at first wanted them to be co-coaches. However, the Coach told him that there should only be one coach, and that Carlos was the coach — end of discussion.

Carlos agreed, and the combination had been awesome. And in Carlos's opening year, the team came in first in their league—much to Carlos' amazement, but not the Coach's.

Chapter 21
Great Leadership:
The Trust Triangle

Aristotle, a great Greek thinker and likely the wisest philosopher of all time, lived more than 2,000 years ago, but his basic lessons live on today as fundamental truths. In his famous book *Rhetoric,* Aristotle explained that for great communicators (orators) to be credible, trustworthy, and persuasive to audiences whom they wanted to move to action, they had to demonstrate to their audiences three distinct personal characteristics: Good Character, Good Sense, and Good Will.

Having worked with leaders in both the private and public sectors for years, I have found Aristotle's advice about what makes a good, trusted leader unsurpassed by that of any other management or leadership thinkers. In short, if leaders want to get anyone to follow them, they must establish trust by demonstrating the same traits that Aristotle taught: Good Character, Good Sense, and Good Will.

It is that simple and that hard!

In the story of *The Trusted Leader,* I presented a simulated case study of what young Carlos Lopez searched to find: Leadership. A clean-slate kind of guy, Carlos had little experience in leading when Jim Talon, the managing partner for the firm, tapped him to take over from a very experienced, idolized, and now-retired leader. In response to this challenge and after some misdirection by Jim Talon, Carlos did the smart thing and looked up his old basketball coach, Jack Dempsey.

The Coach had worked with young men for many years at Arlington High School (a fictitious name) and had ·been the only coach ever to win five consecutive state basketball championships—all after his beloved wife, Emma, died. The relationship between Carlos and the Coach grows as they meet every couple of weeks at Tony's, a small Italian restaurant in town, where Carlos asks questions and the Coach offers his perspective in his typically understated manner. Carlos eagerly absorbs the Coach's solid advice and takes it back to the workplace to test it in the business world.

By contrast, Carlos's boss, Jim Talon, also gave Carlos advice: To go into his new leadership position strong, to take charge, to show them who was boss, make changes—fast. Jim Talon's heavy-handed advice doesn't work in Carlos' case. In fact, Jim's advice (however well meaning) backfires on Carlos. It's not until Carlos finds his own style, after help from the Coach, that Carlos takes flight as an effective leader. Here now follows an explication of the Coach's advice—based on Aristotle's ancient core teachings about what makes a great speaker, and in business, a great leader: Good Character, Good Sense, and Good Will.

Great Leaders and Good Character

The first, primary characteristic of a great leader is Good Character. To explain this one in my presentations, I give examples, and we talk about the Five C's:

1. **Candor:** Telling the truth, even when it hurts, with clients and colleagues, is central to a leader's credibility. In surveys by researchers regarding commonly held values, honesty always comes out number one. Note that telling the truth does not mean you have to be

brutal, for example by saying: "You're a jerk, and people don't respect you!" While such a statement might well be honest, it's so raw that it may create more push-back from the recipient than the intended learning possibly derived from it. Better to ask, "May I offer you an observation about your style?" This may be a better way to step into the water rather than by diving in head first. Here's the follow-up: "Some have described your style as a bit heavy-handed, even at times arrogant—does that sound familiar? Have you ever heard that before?"

2. **Communication:** People need to know what their leaders are thinking. So, tell, write, or text-message them, but let them know—if you want to be an effective leader. Without relevant and timely information, rumors (often-worst-case-scenario types of rumors) abound. With current, reliable information, a sense of being valued and a feeling of stability typically pervade the workplace. Great leaders have this capacity to keep people fully informed. One of the harsher descriptions I have heard colleagues use to describe a bad leader was that he employed the "mushroom theory" to guide his corporate communications policy: "Keep them in the dark and feed them B.S.!" Open, transparent leadership provides the only defense to destructive rumor and innuendo. While being in the inner circle and possessing scarcely held information may feel good at some egotistical level, such exclusivity alienates others, deflates confidence, and in the end, stifles trust and eventually productivity.

3. **Commitment:** People want to know if leaders are in the company for the long haul. Anyone can come into an organization, make a splash, touch a required management base in a career development system, and move on. But the great leaders focus on where they are right now, not how fast they can get to the next place on the corporate ladder.

    A story about the hen and the chicken helps explain this one. One day the hen is scratching in the yard and a pig comes along. The two talk. Over time, the two get to know each other well, become barnyard partners, and decide to throw a party for the other animals in the yard — as a way of demonstrating their appreciation. So, the two discuss a possible menu. One day the hen sees the pig and comes up and says excitedly, "I've finally figured out what we could serve." "Great, what is it?" asks the smiling pig. "Ham and eggs," replies the chicken. It takes a few seconds and the smile melts from the pig's face. The excited chicken couldn't figure out why the pig had suddenly become somber. "You don't seem to like the idea. What's the problem?" The pig looked at the chicken and said, "Think about it...ham and eggs." The chicken looked at him with a blank stare.. So the pig said, "I'll be committed, but you'll just be involved!"

    Ultimately, commitment speaks directly to integrity — leaders doing what they say they would do. And, staying committed to their word isn't always easy for leaders, especially in the face of opposition. However, good reputation gets built on this fierce commitment to our word. Once people believe that leaders will stay committed to their word, there's no place they won't follow.

4. **Consistency:** A leader who is evenhanded, one who plays fairly and consistently, wins the long-distance race of great leadership. Colleagues just want to know that the leader who shows up on day one will be the same person on day two, and so on.. We all want reliability in an effective leader. If you've been around in business, you've had the opportunity to sit on your fair share of employee interview boards. And if you're like I am, you've chosen people who — despite all your behaviorally based questions, recommendations, and class standings — were not the same people after they got hired. It's a reality, albeit a frustrating one. The same is true about new CEOs, new line supervisors, and particularly any leaders placed in charge of profit-and-loss statements. I once had a professor who used to say routinely, "When writing a paper, keep it straightforward — bore me with structure [Consistency]." I think that often in a fast-paced world we want to be unique, but in trying to achieve that goal, we can appear to be inconsistent and scattered. So, as a leader, bore them with your consistency!

5. **Courage:** Doing the right thing, at the right time, for the right reason isn't but it's what great leaders do routinely. Focusing on something of value, something beyond themselves, and having the courage to stand up for it separates great leaders from the rest of the herd. George Washington was revered as a great leader precisely because he consistently answered the call of his country and did what was best for the country, not himself. First as the leader of the Continental Army and then as the first president, Washington always stepped up and did the right thing at the right time, despite his personal convenience, or for

that matter, his personal safety. Courage provides the moral scaffold upon which all other personal characteristics (Candor, Communication, Commitment and Consistency) depend.

Great Leaders and Good Sense

The second characteristic of great leaders is Good Sense. Along with good character, great leaders must also have good sense: Knowledge. Such leaders don't have to be the smartest people in the room but must have knowledge in several specific areas.. I call these five areas of knowledge the Five K's. Thus, as a great leader, you must:

1. **Know Yourself:** In one of his older cowboy movies, Clint Eastwood once said, "A man has to know his limitations." As leaders, men and women need to know what they're good at as well as what they're challenged by. It's sometimes startling how often leaders lack a full sense of self-awareness (how others see them) — which often becomes a major derailer in their careers. Leaders should take time to look deeply into the mirror for their strengths and challenges. One way to do this is to have a 360 degree assessment completed on themselves. Typically their own boss, three to five peers, and three to five direct reports provide their observations in a confidential way to a neutral third party who aggregates the data and presents it to the leader, the client. A simple but effective method to get at the assessment data focuses on four questions: *As a Leader…What do you do well? What do you need to stop doing? What do you need to start doing? And, is there anything else people want to comment on?* Other 360 instruments are very detailed and ask

numerous questions focused on predetermined areas, from how leaders make decisions to how they delegate. In either case, leaders might want an interpretation session from a qualified counselor or executive coach. Daniel Goleman, a leading author on emotional intelligence, says that self-awareness is critical to any successful leader, and the lack of clear self-awareness is like the "live third rail on a train track" — it can electrocute even the smartest of leaders.

2. **Know Others:** Understanding how others think and what their strengths and challenges are is likewise critical to being a great leader. In a study of what employees most wanted — to be appreciated, to be in the know about what's going on, and to be supported in their professional and personal lives — it was eye opening that managers, who were also surveyed had not identified *any* of those items as most likely desired by employees. In other words, managers were clueless about what their direct reports wanted most from them as leaders. Also, Daniel Goleman's research about emotional and social intelligence reflects that along with self-knowledge, knowing others (being empathetic and able to regulate our relationship with others) is critical to being a highly effective leader. Great leaders need to understand those working for them, to ensure that everyone on the team gets to work with his or her strengths most of the time. My personal goal is to have people working no more than fifteen percent of their time in their challenge areas and to spend eighty-five percent of their time in a high-positive, strengths-based state. Thus, if you're a great teacher but not such a wonderful researcher, figure out how to partner with another colleague who

loves to research but needs help in the classroom. That way you both can spend time in areas to which you're individually more suited. Though this makes sense, many leaders spend time balancing their accounting books when they should leave that to the bookkeeper and accountant (though ultimately leaders are responsible for their finances). Spending time at their "highest and best use" will pay off for leaders and for the company.

3. **Know Your Stuff:** Knowing your profession is critical but deserves some explanation. If you're a managing partner of a law firm, you have to be a competent lawyer. You do not have to be the best litigator or probate attorney in the group, but you have to be a competent lawyer, or no one will respect or follow you. This professional competency covers the gamut, from law to medicine and from construction to manufacturing. That's why rapid promotion, based solely on potential and intelligence, is both a disservice to the employee and to the company. Leaders in development require "time in the trenches" learning the craft. In my FBI career, I recall being plucked from the field back to headquarters because I could write. At first it was cool, heady wine, to be writing for the FBI, but when it came to my next field assignment, I had a LOT of learning and experience to gather quickly. There were many days in that first leadership year when I wished I'd had more extensive field experience before taking on that field supervisory position. Fast-tracking of young leaders is often required and will be a reality as more baby boomers leave the workplace en masse. However, be careful to ensure that those fast-trackers don't get derailed from a lack of experience.

4. **Know How to Learn:** In a world that changes so rapidly, leaders who have not learned how to keep up by scheduling learning time will fall behind the knowledge curve and risk becoming irrelevant. New learning systems—online courses, webinars, blogs, social networking—are constantly emerging. Taking time to learn the technology is no longer just a luxury—it's critical to success. Jim Collins in his now-famous book, *Good to Great,* talks about establishing a culture of discipline—disciplined thought, disciplined action, and I would add disciplined education. Learning happens constantly. Children learn language by mimicking, and followers learn leadership by watching leaders. The key: Watch great leaders and study the right cases to get focused and disciplined. I once heard a fellow talk about his twenty-five years of experience as a leader, but when he left the table, another leader piped up: "Really, he only has one year of experience that he's repeated over and over again for twenty-five years!"

5. **Know How to Teach:** One of a leader's primary functions is to ensure a successful future for the team. In a very real sense, good succession planning should be a constant act—not something done behind closed doors every few years. Successful, dynamic, ongoing succession planning can only be accomplished by training and mentoring others to move up and even move out of the organization. Training and development must be viewed as just as important as marketing, advertising, and finance. As companies mature, everyone, from the CEO on down, requires new skills. And the leadership team is responsible for making education happen. Without education and develop-

ment, companies lose the competitive edge. With education, companies flourish.. Lately it's been fascinating to see how many companies have recognized and developed "alumni associations," cultivating groups of former employees with whom they regularly communicate and engage in company activities to preserve and perpetuate knowledge.

Great Leaders and Good Will

The third, final, and often overlooked characteristic of great leaders is Good Will. Along with good character and good sense, great leaders must also have good will toward others. Simply put: Leaders should have the best intentions for those with whom they are working—both colleagues and clients alike. When it comes to good will, I call upon the Five H's, all based on the word "honor." Note that I use the word "honor" rather than "respect," also one of my favorite leadership words. I chose the word "honor" because I think honor implies a degree of humility in respecting another. And the great leaders have this humility and honor-bound tradition in their DNA, as Jim Collins noted in his best seller, *Good to Great*. So, here are the Five H's:

1. **Honor Yourself:** You have to be true to who you are. In fact, such personal integrity (which has been mentioned before under Consistency) shines through as the hallmark of great leaders. They honor themselves by only making choices and decisions consistent with their values and beliefs—who they are as natural, authentic leaders. Here's the test you can take to determine whether or not you're honoring yourself: Would what you're doing make you proud or blush if

it ended up on the evening news? In law this is called the "red-face" test. There may be no explicit law against it, however if such behavior would cause you shame and embarrassment, best to walk away from it. For example, I have always stood up against racism and frankly along the way it has cost me. I've always refused to laugh at racist jokes—and openly express my distaste for them. Refusing to laugh in certain organizations, especially if senior people engage in such hurtful behavior, can cause deep rifts in your career. Some time ago I was interviewing at a client's site for potential business. Seated alone at one point with an older board member of the company, I listened as he told what turned out in the punch line to be a racial joke. When he finished the joke, he roared and hit the table, but I just stared at him with a stern look and proceeded to move on. He was clearly embarrassed, and I was never hired for the coaching job for which I knew I was a good fit (at least until that joke). A great saying I once heard: "Stand for something or you'll fall for anything and stand for nothing." At the end of the day, leaders need to look in the mirror and respect the person they see. All honor starts within before it moves out to the world—like concentric circles that form in a lake when you toss in a rock.

2. **Honor Others:** Leaders get what they give. It's the simple, ancient social rule of reciprocity. Not only do people return what they get, but reciprocity happens for both good (positive) and bad (negative)—leading to both virtuous or vicious cycles. Thus, such double-edged reciprocity helps forge great partnerships or start great wars. It's how we can have, on the one

hand, a Martin Luther King Jr., or on the other, an Adolf Hitler. Honor given first to another always begets honor given back to the donor. Give before you get and see the results. At a basic level, honor everyone you meet and you'll rarely make a mistake. Figuring out people's strengths and challenges helps a leader know how to approach them. I start with what people bring to the table and try to work from there. While trying to "fix" someone sounds logical, such efforts are most often a failed task. However, focusing on a challenge to ensure that it does not derail a leader makes more sense. But staying locked on "fixing" weaknesses at the expense of honoring their strengths presents a fatal leadership flaw. Neither Michael Phelps nor Tiger Woods is ever going to win a major contest by working solely on his weaknesses. Leaders who focus on fixing their teams' weaknesses start at the wrong end of the equation and are doomed to failure. You get what you focus on...so focus on strengths, not weaknesses. As they warn race car drivers: Watch the road ahead, not the wall.

3.   **Honor the Company:** Honor given to the organization for which you work is smart for you, for those you lead, and for the company. While companies need to do the right thing, leaders and employees who honor the mission, vision, and values of a company will always have a good day at work. Employees who treat the company as if they were principal owners, or large stockholders will find themselves paying far more honor to the company than not. I'm not talking about blind loyalty, but a blend of loyalty and reasonable discretion. In the final analysis, the company for many of us is our "other family." Ensuring that we honor

that family, our work family, where we spend most of our adult lives, makes personal as well as but financial sense.

4. **Honor the Community:** Leaders work, live and play in a community that must be honored and supported if all are to be successful. Community is our social glue, just above family and work—as part of the concentric circle of honor. Consider community the critical life-support system for work and even family. The lack of a sense of community has a direct effect on our everyday life. If our surroundings, neighborhoods, and cities are dirty, crime filled, and corrupt, little else can survive, let alone thrive. When communities are not honored, litter, debris, and crime begin to pollute the social oxygen. There's a theory called the "broken windows theory" that says if you let graffiti or broken windows go unfixed, such disregard begets only more destruction. The message that most smart communities have figured out follows: If someone dishonors/defaces property, fix it immediately to send a message that you honor it and will not stand for such dishonor. And to do this, all people have to step up and become civic leaders—whether serving on nonprofit boards or helping out as Big Brothers, Big Sisters, Scout leaders, or whatever we're called upon to do to make the community a better place.

5. **Honor the Country and the World:** At the highest level of the concentric circle of honor, we are all part of a global society (a flatter world than we ever imagined) and need to honor both our own country and the greater world. We're all seeing, every day, how the environment and the economy are interdependent. By

honoring our country and the world, we not only insure freedom and health for ourselves but also for our children and grandchildren. Honor can come in many forms, not the least of which is philanthropy — the love of mankind. An ultimate source of respect, philanthropy directed at our community, country, and world says "I honor you." Remember how reciprocity works — it comes back to you in equal measure. Look at the reciprocity England has given the United States since our help to them in World War II. People, organizations, and countries remember when you honor them and will repay in kind. Finally, all of us, no matter how great or small, eventually need help. So start with honor, and it will follow you around for a lifetime.

Some Final Words

Final Notes about the Trust Triangle:

To have highest trust, great leaders must possess significant levels of strength in all three attributes of The Trust Triangle: Good Character, Good Sense, and Good Will. Most of us will not have—at the highest levels, at all times—all the 5C's (Candor, Communication, Commitment, Consistency and Courage); the 5K's (Know: Self, Others, the Job, how to Learn and how to Teach); and the 5H's (Honor: Self, Others, Company, Community, Country and World). Thus, like most important issues in life, pursuing these elements of The Trust Triangle will be a lifetime journey for us all. Finally, developing only one or two sides of The Trust Triangle will not work—The Triangle will collapse. We MUST develop all three sides to become great leaders. I wish you well on your journey.

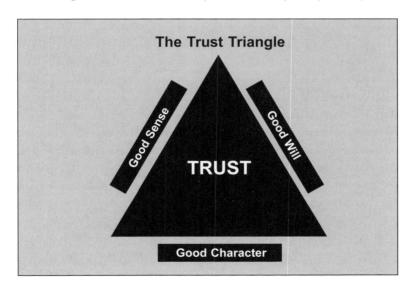

Other Books by Steve Gladis

The Transparent Leader: Effective Leadership Communication (HRD Press, 2009)

Written as a business leadership fable, *The Transparent Leader* is the story of a smart emerging leader, Stephanie Marcus, as she navigates the challenging world of business. fortunately, Steph meets Lou Donaldson, a public relations CEO near the end of his career, at a local gym where she works out daily. Lou acts as a friend, informal coach, and mentor as he guides Steph through the complicated business ecosystem in which she finds herself. Throughout the story, Steph learns about clear leadership communication as she also adapts and changes and becomes a more transparent—clear and open—leader. At the same time, she learns Lou's personal story, which helps her fully appreciate his wisdom.

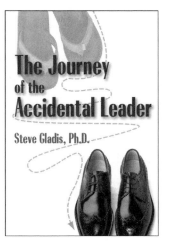

The Journey of the Accidental Leader (HRD Press, October 2007)

Written as a business fable, *The Journey of the Accidental Leader* is the story of a young man who, like so many people, gets thrust into a leadership position he neither wanted nor asked for. What he does and how he reacts makes the book both entertaining and informative. This book is based on the author's practical leadership experience as a Marine Corps officer in Vietnam.

The Executive Coach in the Corporate Forest (HRD Press, July 2008)

Foreword by Marshall Goldsmith, the world's leading executive coach. A business fable, *The Executive Coach in the Corporate Forest* is the story of a young, gifted executive coach, J. C. Williams, and his coaching relationships with his rather varied and interesting business clients — all with their own challenges. The book offers some engaging stories, has believable characters with realistic problems, and illustrates the structure and content of the coaching process. The book is a quick read and was written to explain the coaching process to executives who didn't understand it.

Survival Writing for Business (HRD Press, May 2005)

To write well, you need to keep it clear and concise. This book shows how and is a no-nonsense, virtual lifeline to writing success.

The Manager's Pocket Guide to Public Presentations (HRD Press, March 1999)

This book is an indispensable reference for managers and executives who find themselves in the unfamiliar and often frightening position of having to give a public presentation. It is a compendium of tips that will help any manager learn the survival tactics of public speaking. A simple, quick read, based on the accepted theory and practice of rhetoric, it is also a confidence builder that will help any manager begin to overcome anxiety over public speaking.

Manager's Pocket Guide to Effective Writing (HRD Press, January 1999)

Written communication is prevalent at most levels of business, but especially at the managerial level. Your writing may be grammatically and logically sound, but is it effective? Is it conveying your message with the concision and accuracy that makes you an effective communicator? Whether you're a manager in charge of a group of writers, or just a person interested in improving his or her writing skills, *The Manager's Pocket Guide to Effective Writing* uses easy, practical, how-to steps to help you write better and ultimately make a better impression on others.

Writetype: Personality Types and Writing Styles (HRD Press, June 1994)

Based on individual personality styles, this book provides new strategies for the four basic types of writers: the correspondent, the technical writer, the creative writer, and the analytical writer. Each person fits one of these well-defined writing "types." Once readers learn their writing personality and follow the writing process suggested in the book, they find writing easier and less anxiety-producing.

Leadership Blog: Survival Leadership http://survivalleadership.blogspot.com. This leadership blog intends to help leaders achieve success though a series of video lectures, book reviews, and even humor about leadership development.

How to reach the author:
Contact the author via e-mail (sgladis@stevegladis.com) or visit his website (www.SteveGladis.com).